THE
ESSENTIAL
WISDOM
OF THE
WORLD'S
GREATEST
THINKERS

THE
ESSENTIAL
WISDOM
OF THE
WORLD'S
GREATEST
THINKERS

edited by
CAROL KELLY-GANGI

FALL RIVER PRESS

New York

FALL RIVER PRESS

New York

An Imprint of Sterling Publishing Co., Inc.
1166 Avenue of the Americas
New York, NY 10036

Compilation © 2016 Sterling Publishing Co., Inc.

ISBN 978-1-4351-6195-5

Distributed in Canada by Sterling Publishing Co., Inc.
c/o Canadian Manda Group, 664 Annette Street
Toronto, Ontario, Canada M6S 2C8
Distributed in the United Kingdom by GMC Distribution Services
Castle Place, 166 High Street, Lewes, East Sussex, England BN7 1XU
Distributed in Australia by NewSouth Books
45 Beach Street, Coogee, NSW 2034, Australia

For information about custom editions, special sales, and premium
and corporate purchases, please contact Sterling Special Sales
at 800-805-5489 or specialsales@sterlingpublishing.com.

Manufactured in the United States of America

4   6   8   10   9   7   5   3

sterlingpublishing.com

Cover design by David Ter-Avanesyan
Book design by Rich Hazelton

CONTENTS

❋ ❋ ❋ ❋ ❋

In loving memory of my father
Howard Kelly
who is forever in my heart

INTRODUCTION

❋   ❋   ❋   ❋   ❋

Where is the knowledge we have lost in information?

—T. S. Eliot

It's a reality of life in the digital age that we are bombarded with information during every waking moment. Our relentless quest for up-to-the-minute news on everything from the globally important to the utterly mundane can be insidiously addictive. Why not take a step back from the dizzying amount of information and peruse the words of some of the greatest thinkers the world has ever known? *The Essential Wisdom of the World's Greatest Thinkers* is just that—a sampling of quotations from the extraordinary men and women who have shaped our world from antiquity up through the present day.

Who are these profound thinkers? Represented in these pages you will find philosophers and scholars; artists and writers; poets and politicians; religious leaders and world leaders; saints and scientists; musicians and orators; and actors and activists. It is hoped that the words of these great thinkers form a living dialogue of ideas which crosses the boundaries of time and place. Aristotle, Albert Einstein, John F. Kennedy, Margaret Mead, and Gloria Steinem exchange ideas on the pursuit of knowledge. Elsewhere, Mahatma Gandhi, Thomas Jefferson, Abraham Lincoln, John Locke, Nelson Mandela, Voltaire, and Simone Weil extol the primacy of freedom and liberty. Albert Camus, Euripides, Helen Keller, Eleanor Roosevelt, and Booker T. Washington each offer their firmly held beliefs on the key to happiness. While Maya Angelou, Pope Francis, Sophocles, and Elie Wiesel share their insights into the meaning of hardship, adversity, and hope. In many ways the selections are as singular as the speakers themselves, yet there are a number of universal themes that are revealed: the enduring love for family and friends; the fervent desire for peace among peoples and nations; the endless struggle for equality and justice; the curious nature of politics; the majesty of the arts; the wonder of science and technology; and the role of religion, morality, and virtue in our lives and in our world.

It is my hope that spending some time with these great thinkers—from Aristotle to Yeats—who have each left an indelible mark on our world will help to inform, inspire, and challenge us as we continue on our own life's journey toward wisdom.

—CAROL KELLY-GANGI
2016

KNOWLEDGE, LEARNING, AND EDUCATION

All men by nature desire knowledge.

—**Aristotle**

❧

Man is obviously made for thinking. Therein lies all his dignity and his merit; and his whole duty is to think as he ought.

—**Blaise Pascal**

❧

I think, therefore I am.

—**René Descartes**

❧

It is not our body which feels, not our mind which thinks, but we, as single human beings, who both feel and think.

—**St. Thomas Aquinas**

The human mind has a desire to know its place in the universe and the role we play in the tapestry of life. This is actually hardwired into our brains, the desire to know our relationship to the universe.

—**Michio Kaku**

❦

The first duty of a man is the seeking after and the investigation of truth.

—**Cicero**

❦

The key to good decision making is not knowledge. It is understanding. We are swimming in the former. We are desperately lacking in the latter.

—**Malcolm Gladwell**

❦

Knowledge will forever govern ignorance; and a people who mean to be their own governors must arm themselves with the power which knowledge gives.

—**James Madison**

❦

The pursuit of knowledge itself implies a world where men are free to follow out the logic of their own ideas. It implies a world where nations are free to solve their own problems and to realize their own ideals.

—**John F. Kennedy**

❦

Knowledge is of no value unless you put it into practice.

—**Anton Chekhov**

If you have knowledge, let others light their candles in it.

—**Margaret Fuller**

Ignorance, the root and stem of all evil.

—**Plato**

There is only one good, namely, knowledge; and only one evil, namely, ignorance.

—**Socrates**

Knowledge itself is power.

—**Francis Bacon**

Where is the knowledge we have lost in information?

—**T. S. Eliot**

I was brought up to believe that the only thing worth doing was to add to the sum of accurate information in the world.

—**Margaret Mead**

Learning is not attained by chance, it must be sought for with ardor and attended to with diligence.

—**Abigail Adams**

I wanted to know the name of every stone and flower and insect and bird and beast. I wanted to know where it got its color, where it got its life—but there was no one to tell me.

—George Washington Carver

By three methods we may learn wisdom: first, by reflection, which is noblest; second, by imitation, which is easiest; and third by experience, which is the bitterest.

—Confucius

Everywhere, we learn only from those whom we love.

—Goethe

The important thing is not to stop questioning.

—Albert Einstein

The learner always begins by finding fault, but the scholar sees the positive merit in everything.

—Georg Hegel

It is the province of knowledge to speak, and it is the privilege of wisdom to listen.

—Oliver Wendell Holmes, Sr.

A mind is a fire to be kindled, not a vessel to be filled.

—**Plutarch**

❧

An intellectual is someone whose mind watches itself.

—**Albert Camus**

❧

I want to tell you how welcome you are to the White House.
I think this is the most extraordinary collection of talent, of human
knowledge, that has ever been gathered together at the White
House, with the possible exception of when Thomas Jefferson
dined alone.

—**John F. Kennedy, remarks honoring
Nobel Prize winners, April 29, 1962**

❧

As every divided kingdom falls, so every mind divided between many
studies confounds and saps itself.

—**Leonardo da Vinci**

❧

How wearisome the grammarian, the phrenologist, the political or
religious fanatic, or indeed any possessed mortal whose balance is lost
by the exaggeration of a single topic.

—**Ralph Waldo Emerson**

The first problem for all of us, men and women, is not to learn, but to unlearn.

—Gloria Steinem

༄

We cannot learn without pain.

—Aristotle

༄

Anybody who has survived his childhood has enough information about life to last him the rest of his days.

—Flannery O'Connor

༄

Experience: that most brutal of teachers. But you learn, my God do you learn.

—C. S. Lewis

༄

You will ever remember that all the end of study is to make you a good man and a useful citizen.

—John Adams

༄

My alma mater was books, a good library . . . I could spend the rest of my life reading, just satisfying my curiosity.

—Malcolm X

Once you learn to read, you will be forever free.

—**Frederick Douglass**

❧

I am a part of everything that I have read.

—**Theodore Roosevelt**

❧

The world exists for the education of each man.

—**Ralph Waldo Emerson**

❧

It is the mark of an educated mind to be able to entertain a thought without accepting it.

—**Aristotle**

❧

Education is an admirable thing, but it is well to remember from time to time that nothing that is worth knowing can be taught.

—**Oscar Wilde**

❧

Education is the point at which we decide whether we love the world enough to assume responsibility for it and by the same token save it from that ruin which, except for renewal, except for the coming of the new and young, would be inevitable.

—**Hannah Arendt**

Education is the ability to listen to almost anything without losing your temper or your self-confidence.

—**Robert Frost**

Education is the most powerful weapon which you can use to change the world.

—**Nelson Mandela**

It requires troublesome work to undertake the alteration of old beliefs.

—**John Dewey**

To educate a person in mind and not in morals is to educate a menace to society.

—**Theodore Roosevelt**

Educating the mind without educating the heart is no education at all.

—**Aristotle**

What usually happens in the educational process is that the faculties are dulled, overloaded, stuffed and paralyzed so that by the time most people are mature they have lost their innate capabilities.

—**R. Buckminster Fuller**

The purpose of education is to replace an empty mind with an open one.

—Malcolm Forbes

Education is not preparation for life; education is life itself.

—John Dewey

When asked how much educated men were superior to those uneducated, Aristotle answered, "As much as the living are to the dead."

—Diogenes Laërtius

Upon the subject of education, not presuming to dictate any plan or system respecting it, I can only say that I view it as the most important subject which we as a people can be engaged in.

—Abraham Lincoln

Education is a complex, multifaceted, and painstaking process, and being gifted does not make this less so.

—Terence Tao

One's work may be finished some day, but one's education never!

—Alexandre Dumas

Life is my college. May I graduate well, and earn some honors!

—Louisa May Alcott

We are all teachers and students of ourselves.

—A. Bartlett Giamatti

IMAGINATION, INNOVATION, AND TECHNOLOGY

The mightiest lever known to the moral world,
    Imagination.

—**William Wordsworth**

❧

Without leaps of imagination or dreaming, we lose the excitement of
possibilities. Dreaming, after all, is a form of planning.

—**Gloria Steinem**

❧

Imagination is more important than knowledge. For knowledge is
limited, whereas imagination embraces the entire world, stimulating
progress, giving birth to evolution. It is, strictly speaking, a real factor
in scientific research. Imagination circles the world.

—**Albert Einstein**

He who has imagination without learning has wings and no feet.

—Joseph Joubert

❧

The imagination should be allowed a certain amount of time to browse around.

—Thomas Merton

❧

Man is a shrewd inventor, and is ever taking the hint of a new machine from his own structure, adapting some secret of his own anatomy in iron, wood, and leather, to some required function in the work of the world.

—Ralph Waldo Emerson

❧

Daring ideas are like chessmen moved forward; they may be beaten, but they may start a winning game.

—Goethe

❧

Nothing in progression can rest on its original plan. We may as well think of rocking a grown man in the cradle of an infant.

—Edmund Burke

❧

I'm obsessive about imagination and the link from imagination to the sense of possibility.

—Maxine Greene

Ideas are like rabbits. You get a couple and learn how to handle them, and pretty soon you have a dozen.

—**John Steinbeck**

∾

If one is accustomed to easy success, one may not develop the patience necessary to deal with truly difficult problems. Talent is important, of course; but how one develops and nurtures it is even more so.

—**Terence Tao**

∾

To invent, you need a good imagination and a pile of junk.

—**Thomas Edison**

∾

A man may die, nations may rise and fall, but an idea lives on.

—**John F. Kennedy**

∾

The ultimate creative thinking technique is to think like God. If you're an atheist, pretend how God would do it.

—**Frank Lloyd Wright**

∾

Anyone who stops learning is old, whether at twenty or eighty. Anyone who keeps learning stays young. The greatest thing in life is to keep your mind young.

—**Henry Ford**

No great genius has ever existed without some touch of madness.

—**Aristotle**

❧

With copious evidence ranging from Plato's haughtiness to Beethoven's tirades, we may conclude that the most brilliant people of history tend to be a prickly lot.

—**Stephen Jay Gould**

❧

People of humor are always in some degree people of genius.

—**Samuel Taylor Coleridge**

❧

I was taught that the way of progress was neither swift nor easy.

—**Marie Curie**

❧

I'm convinced that about half of what separates the successful entrepreneurs from the non-successful ones is pure perseverance.

—**Steve Jobs**

❧

When a true genius appears in this world, you may know him by this sign, that the dunces are all in confederacy against him.

—**Jonathan Swift**

We must not forget that when radium was discovered no one knew that it would prove useful in hospitals. The work was one of pure science. And this is a proof that scientific work must not be considered from the point of view of the direct usefulness of it.

—Marie Curie

If we had a reliable way to label our toys good and bad, it would be easy to regulate technology wisely. But we can rarely see far enough ahead to know which road leads to damnation. Whoever concerns himself with big technology, either to push it forward or to stop it, is gambling in human lives.

—Freeman Dyson

The empires of the future are the empires of the mind.

—Winston Churchill

Our inventions are wont to be pretty toys, which distract our attention from serious things. They are but improved means to an unimproved end.

—Henry David Thoreau

We live in a society exquisitely dependent on science and technology, in which hardly anyone knows anything about science and technology.

—Carl Sagan

You can't just ask customers what they want and then try to give that to them. By the time you get it built, they'll want something new.

—Steve Jobs

Any science or technology which is sufficiently advanced is indistinguishable from magic.

—Arthur C. Clarke

Technology is nothing. What's important is that you have a faith in people, that they're basically good and smart, and if you give them tools, they'll do wonderful things with them.

—Steve Jobs

Man is still the most extraordinary computer of all.

—John F. Kennedy

When I took office, only high energy physicists had ever heard of what is called the World Wide Web. . . . Now even my cat has its own page.

—Bill Clinton

We are all now connected by the Internet, like neurons in a giant brain.

—Stephen Hawking

Never before in history has innovation offered promise of so much to so many in so short a time.

—**Bill Gates**

All of us must recognize that education and innovation will be the currency of the twenty-first century.

—**Barack Obama**

LOVE AND KINDNESS

One word frees us of all the weight and pain in life. That word is Love.

—Socrates

∾

Love is life. All, everything that I understand, I understand only because I love. Everything is, everything exists, only because I love. Everything is united by it alone. Love is God, and to die means that I, a particle of love, shall return to the general and eternal source.

—Leo Tolstoy

∾

How bold one gets when one is sure of being loved!

—Sigmund Freud

∾

Where there is great love, there are always miracles.

—Willa Cather

Love, by reason of its passion, destroys the in-between which relates us to and separates us from others. As long as its spell lasts, the only in-between which can insert itself between two lovers is the child, love's own product.

—Hannah Arendt

∾

True love is both loving and letting oneself be loved. It is harder to let ourselves be loved than it is to love.

—Pope Francis

∾

The magic of first love is our ignorance that it can never end.

—Benjamin Disraeli

∾

Love is of all passions the strongest, for it attacks simultaneously the head, the heart, and the senses.

—Lao Tzu

∾

Love is a serious mental disease.

—Plato

∾

Love is composed of a single soul inhabiting two bodies.

—Aristotle

Love is the only force capable of transforming an enemy into a friend.

—**Martin Luther King, Jr.**

Love makes your soul crawl out from its hiding place.

—**Zora Neale Hurston**

Being deeply loved by someone gives you strength, while loving someone deeply gives you courage.

—**Lao Tzu**

There is hardly any activity, any enterprise, which is started out with such tremendous hopes and expectations, and yet which fails so regularly, as love.

—**Erich Fromm**

Many people when they fall in love look for a little haven of refuge from the world, where they can be sure of being admired when they are not admirable, and praised when they are not praiseworthy.

—**Bertrand Russell**

Find the person who will love you because of your differences and not in spite of them and you have found a lover for life.

—**Leo Buscaglia**

Among those whom I like or admire, I can find no common denominator, but among those whom I love, I can: All of them make me laugh.

—**W. H. Auden**

To love and win is the best thing. To love and lose is the next best.

—**William Makepeace Thackeray**

There is no remedy for love but to love more.

—**Henry David Thoreau**

Better to have loved and lost, than to have never loved at all.

—**St. Augustine**

We are shaped and fashioned by what we love.

—**Goethe**

If you judge people, you have no time to love them.

—**Mother Teresa**

The little unremembered acts of kindness and love are the best parts of a person's life.

—**William Wordsworth**

What does love look like? It has the hands to help others. It has the feet to hasten to the poor and needy. It has eyes to see misery and want. It has the ears to hear the sighs and sorrows of men. That is what love looks like.

—St. Augustine

Love is so short, forgetting is so long.

—Pablo Neruda

Don't hold to anger, hurt or pain. They steal your energy and keep you from love.

—Leo Buscaglia

You learn to speak by speaking, to study by studying, to run by running, to work by working; and just so, you learn to love by loving. All those who think to learn in any other way deceive themselves.

—St. Francis de Sales

Love never dies a natural death. It dies because we don't know how to replenish its source. It dies of blindness and errors and betrayals. It dies of illness and wounds; it dies of weariness, of witherings, of tarnishings.

—Anaïs Nin

Darkness cannot drive out darkness; only light can do that. Hate cannot drive out hate; only love can do that.

—**Martin Luther King, Jr.**

❧

For one human being to love another: that is perhaps the most difficult of our tasks; the ultimate, the last test and proof, the work for which all other work is but preparation.

—**Rainer Maria Rilke**

❧

How far you go in life depends on your being tender with the young, compassionate with the aged, sympathetic with the striving and tolerant of the weak and strong. Because someday in your life you will have been all of these.

—**George Washington Carver**

❧

No one is born hating another person because of the color of his skin, or his background, or his religion. People must learn to hate, and if they can learn to hate, they can be taught to love, for love comes more naturally to the human heart than its opposite.

—**Nelson Mandela**

❧

Be kind, for everyone you meet is fighting a harder battle.

—**Plato**

Kindness in words creates confidence.
Kindness in thinking creates profoundness.
Kindness in giving creates love.

—Lao Tzu

A small act is worth a million thoughts.

—Ai Weiwei

Love and compassion are necessities, not luxuries. Without them, humanity cannot survive.

—Dalai Lama

What do we live for, if it is not to make life less difficult for each other?

—George Eliot

A person who practices compassion and forgiveness has great inner strength, whereas aggression is usually a sign of weakness.

—Dalai Lama

The worst sin towards our fellow creatures is not to hate them but to be indifferent to them; that's the essence of inhumanity.

—George Bernard Shaw

There is a wisdom of the head, and a wisdom of the heart.

—**Charles Dickens**

❧

I shall pass through this world but once. Any good therefore that I can do or any kindness that I can show to any human being, let me do it now. Let me not defer or neglect it, for I shall not pass this way again.

—**Mahatma Gandhi**

MARRIAGE, FAMILY, AND FRIENDSHIP

The ideal that marriage aims at is that of spiritual union through the physical. The human love that it incarnates is intended to serve as a stepping stone to divine or universal love.

—**Mahatma Gandhi**

❧

There is no more lovely, friendly and charming relationship, communion or company than a good marriage.

—**Martin Luther**

❧

I think people are happier in marriage when neither one is the boss, but when both of them are willing to give as well as take.

—**Eleanor Roosevelt**

Happiness in marriage is entirely a matter of chance.

—Jane Austen

&

If there is such a thing as a good marriage, it is because it resembles friendship rather than love.

—Montaigne

&

A good marriage is where both people feel like they're getting the better end of the deal.

—Anne Lamott

&

A good marriage is one which allows for change and growth in the individuals and in the way they express their love.

—Pearl S. Buck

&

At the beginning of a marriage ask yourself whether this woman will be interesting to talk to from now until old age.

—Friedrich Nietzsche

&

By all means, marry. If you get a good wife, you'll become happy; if you get a bad one, you'll become a philosopher.

—Socrates

No man or woman really knows what perfect love is until they have been married a quarter of a century.

—Mark Twain

It takes patience to appreciate domestic bliss; volatile spirits prefer unhappiness.

—George Santayana

It is not a lack of love, but a lack of friendship that makes unhappy marriages.

—Friedrich Nietzsche

When a marriage ends, who is left to understand it?

—Joyce Carol Oates

The person who tries to live alone will not succeed as a human being. His heart withers if it does not answer another heart. His mind shrinks away if he hears only the echoes of his own thoughts and finds no other inspiration.

—Pearl S. Buck

One of the oldest human needs is having someone to wonder where you are when you don't come home at night.

—Margaret Mead

Man is a social animal.

—Benedict de Spinoza

It is not good for man to be alone.

—Jean-Jacques Rousseau

Parenthood changes one's world. It's almost like a switch gets flipped inside you, and you can feel a whole new range of feelings that you never thought you'd have.

—Steve Jobs

A mother's love for her child is like nothing else in the world. It knows no law, no pity, it dares all things and crushes down remorselessly all that stands in its path.

—Agatha Christie

Childrearing is above all an ethical responsibility.

—Steven Pinker

Respect the child. Be not too much his parent. Trespass not on his solitude.

—Ralph Waldo Emerson

It makes no small difference, then, whether we form habits of one kind or of another from our very youth; it makes a very great difference, or rather all the difference.

—**Aristotle**

We are linked by blood, and blood is memory without language.

—**Joyce Carol Oates**

Children have never been very good at listening to their elders, but they have never failed to imitate them.

—**James Baldwin**

The surest way to make your child unhappy is to accustom him to get everything he wants.

—**Jean-Jacques Rousseau**

There's only one thing we can be sure of, and that is the love that we have for our children, for our families, for each other. The warmth of a small child's embrace, that is true.

—**Barack Obama**

The sun looks down on nothing half so good as a household laughing together over a meal.

—**C. S. Lewis**

Happy or unhappy, families are all mysterious. We have only to imagine how differently we would be described—and will be, after our deaths—by each of the family members who believe they know us.

—Gloria Steinem

❧

All happy families resemble one another, but each unhappy family is unhappy in its own way.

—Leo Tolstoy

❧

There is no more precious experience in life than friendship. And I am not forgetting love and marriage as I write this; the lovers, or the man and wife, who are not friends are but weakly joined together.

—Eleanor Roosevelt

❧

What is a friend? A single soul dwelling in two bodies.

—Aristotle

❧

A friend is a gift you give yourself.

—Robert Louis Stevenson

❧

The only reward of virtue is virtue; the only way to have a friend is to be one.

—Ralph Waldo Emerson

True friendship consists not in the multitude of friends but in their worth and value.

—Ben Jonson

They cherish each other's hopes. They are kind to each other's dreams.

—Henry David Thoreau

Friendship marks a life even more deeply than love. Love risks degenerating into obsession, friendship is never anything but sharing.

—Elie Wiesel

A woman may very well form a friendship with a man, but for this to endure, it must be assisted by a little physical antipathy.

—Friedrich Nietzsche

If I were forced to choose between my country and my friend, I hope I would be brave enough to choose my friend.

—E. M. Forster

Only solitary men know the full joys of friendship. Others have their family; but to a solitary and an exile his friends are everything.

—Willa Cather

The glory of friendship is not the outstretched hand, not the kindly smile, nor the joy of companionship; it is the spiritual inspiration that comes to one when you discover that someone else believes in you and is willing to trust you with a friendship.

—**Ralph Waldo Emerson**

Friendship makes prosperity more shining and lessens adversity by dividing and sharing it.

—**Cicero**

I felt it shelter to speak to you.

—**Emily Dickinson**

I don't need a friend who changes when I change and who nods when I nod; my shadow does that much better.

—**Plutarch**

Misfortune shows those who are not really friends.

—**Aristotle**

Consult your friend on all things, especially on those which respect yourself. His counsel may then be useful where your own self-love might impair your judgment.

—**Seneca**

As a matter of self-preservation, a man needs good friends or ardent enemies, for the former instruct him and the latter take him to task.

—Diogenes Laërtius

Don't walk behind me; I may not lead. Don't walk in front of me; I may not follow. Just walk beside me and be my friend.

—Albert Camus

Who hears me, who understands me, become mine,—a possession for all time.

—Ralph Waldo Emerson

For without friends, no one would choose to live, though he had all other goods.

—Aristotle

One of the most beautiful qualities of true friendship is to understand and to be understood.

—Seneca

FREEDOM AND RIGHTS

Men being, as has been said, by nature, all free, equal, and independent, no one can be put out of this estate, and subjected to the political power of another, without his own consent.

—John Locke

Man is born free; and everywhere he is in chains. One thinks himself the master of others, and still remains a greater slave than they.

—Jean-Jacques Rousseau

Liberty has never come from the government. Liberty has always come from the subjects of the government. The history of liberty is a history of resistance. The history of liberty is a history of the limitations of governmental power, not the increase of it.

—Woodrow Wilson

We are not to expect to be translated from despotism to liberty in a featherbed.

—**Thomas Jefferson**

So long as the people do not care to exercise their freedom, those who wish to tyrannize will do so; for tyrants are active and ardent, and will devote themselves in the name of any number of gods, religious and otherwise, to put shackles upon sleeping men.

—**Voltaire**

The people are the only sure reliance for the preservation of our liberty.

—**Thomas Jefferson**

Those who deny freedom to others deserve it not for themselves.

—**Abraham Lincoln**

The moment the slave resolves that he will no longer be a slave, his fetters fall. He frees himself and shows the way to others. Freedom and slavery are mental states.

—**Mahatma Gandhi**

None who have always been free can understand the terrible fascinating power of the hope of freedom to those who are not free.

—**Pearl S. Buck**

I have sworn upon the altar of God, eternal hostility against every form of tyranny over the mind of man.

—Thomas Jefferson

Let us dare to read, think, speak and write.

—John Adams

Lock up your libraries if you like; but there is no gate, no lock, no bolt that you can set upon the freedom of my mind.

—Virginia Woolf

What is freedom of expression? Without the freedom to offend, it ceases to exist.

—Salman Rushdie

I disapprove of what you say, but I will defend to the death your right to say it.

—Voltaire

Freedom is not worth having if it does not include the freedom to make mistakes.

—Mahatma Gandhi

I believe there are more instances of the abridgment of the freedom of the people by gradual and silent encroachments of those in power than by violent and sudden usurpations.

—**James Madison**

❧

The greatest dangers to liberty lurk in insidious encroachment by men of zeal, well-meaning but without understanding.

—**Louis D. Brandeis**

❧

Those who would give up essential liberty to purchase a little temporary safety deserve neither Liberty nor Safety.

—**Franklin D. Roosevelt**

❧

The true danger is when liberty is nibbled away, for expedience, and by parts.

—**Edmund Burke**

❧

Liberty and peace are living things. In each generation—if they are to be maintained—they must be guarded and vitalized anew.

—**Franklin D. Roosevelt**

❧

Freedom is fragile and must be protected. To sacrifice it, even as a temporary measure, is to betray it.

—**Germaine Greer**

Freedom is the very essence of our economy and society. Without freedom the human mind is prevented from unleashing its creative force. But what is also clear is that this freedom does not stand alone. It is freedom in responsibility and freedom to exercise responsibility.

—**Angela Merkel**

To deny people their human rights is to challenge their very humanity.

—**Nelson Mandela**

The best way to enhance freedom in other lands is to demonstrate here that our democratic system is worthy of emulation.

—**Jimmy Carter**

Human beings the world over need freedom and security that they may be able to realize their full potential.

—**Aung San Suu Kyi**

For to be free is not merely to cast off one's chains, but to live in a way that respects and enhances the freedom of others.

—**Nelson Mandela**

Liberty, taking the word in its concrete sense, consists in the ability to choose.

—**Simone Weil**

Freedom means the supremacy of human rights everywhere. Our support goes to those who struggle to gain those rights or keep them.

—**Franklin D. Roosevelt**

The rights of every man are diminished when the rights of one man are threatened.

—**John F. Kennedy**

Men, their rights and nothing more; women, their rights and nothing less.

—**Susan B. Anthony**

Human rights are women's rights, and women's rights are human rights. Let us not forget that among those rights are the right to speak freely—and the right to be heard.

—**Hillary Clinton**

Human rights are not only violated by terrorism, repression or assassination, but also by unfair economic structures that creates huge inequalities.

—**Pope Francis**

EQUALITY, LAW,
AND JUSTICE

If liberty and equality, as is thought by some, are chiefly to be found in democracy, they will be best attained when all persons alike share in government to the utmost.

—Aristotle

We hold these truths to be self-evident, that all men are created equal, that they are endowed by their Creator with certain unalienable Rights, that among these are Life, Liberty, and the pursuit of Happiness.

—Thomas Jefferson

The cost of liberty is less than the price of repression.

—W. E. B. Du Bois

Four score and seven years ago our fathers brought forth on this continent, a new nation, conceived in Liberty, and dedicated to the proposition that all men are created equal.

—**Abraham Lincoln**

We first crush people to the earth, and then claim the right of trampling on them forever, because they are prostrate.

—**Lydia Maria Child**

We hold these truths to be self-evident, that all men and women are created equal.

—**Elizabeth Cady Stanton**

We ask justice, we ask equality, we ask that all civil and political rights that belong to the citizens of the United States be guaranteed to us and our daughters forever.

—**Susan B. Anthony**

As long as you keep a person down, some part of you has to be down there to hold him down, so it means you cannot soar as you otherwise might.

—**Marian Anderson**

You can't hold a man down without staying down with him.

—**Booker T. Washington**

We have talked long enough in this country about equal rights. It is time now to write the next chapter—and to write it in the books of law.

—**Lyndon B. Johnson**

There is all the difference in the world between treating people equally and attempting to make them equal.

—**Friedrich August von Hayek**

There is in this world no such force as the force of a person determined to rise. The human soul cannot be permanently chained.

—**W. E. B. Du Bois**

We all should know that diversity makes for a rich tapestry, and we must understand that all the threads of the tapestry are equal in value no matter what their color.

—**Maya Angelou**

A feminist is anyone who recognizes the equality and full humanity of women and men.

—**Gloria Steinem**

Until we get equality in education, we won't have an equal society.

—Sonia Sotomayor

Women will have achieved true equality when men share with them the responsibility of bringing up the next generation.

—Ruth Bader Ginsburg

Let us remember we are all part of one American family. We are united in common values, and that includes belief in equality under the law, basic respect for public order, and the right of peaceful protest.

—Barack Obama

The good of the people is the greatest law.

—Cicero

Let every American, every lover of liberty, every well wisher to his posterity, swear by the blood of the Revolution, never to violate in the least particular, the laws of the country; and never to tolerate their violation by others.

—Abraham Lincoln

Good people do not need laws to tell them to act responsibly, while bad people will find a way around the laws.

—**Plato**

It seems to me that most men have received from nature enough common sense to make laws, but that everyone is not just enough to make good laws.

—**Voltaire**

Laws, like houses, lean on one another.

—**Edmund Burke**

Laws are like sausages, it is better not to see them being made.

—**Otto von Bismarck**

Wise people, even though all laws were abolished, would still lead the same life.

—**Aristophanes**

If you must break the law, do it to seize power: in all other cases observe it.

—**Julius Caesar**

Laws control the lesser man...Right conduct controls the greater one.

—**Mark Twain**

❧

No written law has ever been more binding than unwritten custom supported by popular opinion.

—**Carrie Chapman Catt**

❧

The foundation of justice, moreover, is good faith;—that is, truth and fidelity to promises and agreements.

—**Cicero**

❧

That old law about "an eye for an eye" leaves everyone blind.

—**Martin Luther King, Jr.**

❧

Justice is conscience, not a personal conscience but the conscience of the whole of humanity.

—**Aleksandr Solzhenitsyn**

❧

If you are neutral in situations of injustice, you have chosen the side of the oppressor. If an elephant has its foot on the tail of a mouse, and you say that you are neutral, the mouse will not appreciate your neutrality.

—**Desmond Tutu**

Judging from the main portions of the history of the world, so far, justice is always in jeopardy.

—**Walt Whitman**

❧

I have always found that mercy bears richer fruits than strict justice.

—**Abraham Lincoln**

❧

If we do not maintain Justice, Justice will not maintain us.

—**Aristotle**

❧

Injustice anywhere is a threat to justice everywhere.

—**Martin Luther King, Jr.**

❧

Where justice is denied, where poverty is enforced, where ignorance prevails, and where any one class is made to feel that society is in an organized conspiracy to oppress, rob, and degrade them, neither persons nor property will be safe.

—**Frederick Douglass**

❧

Ignorance, allied with power, is the most ferocious enemy justice can have.

—**James Baldwin**

Never forget that justice is what love looks like in public.

—**Cornel West**

Justice is indiscriminately due to all, without regard to numbers, wealth, or rank.

—**John Jay**

GOVERNMENT AND POLITICS

The care of human life and happiness, and not their destruction, is the first and only object of good government.

—Thomas Jefferson

The ultimate aim of government is to free every man from fear, that he may live in all possible security. In fact, the true aim of government is liberty.

—Benedict de Spinoza

Why has government been instituted at all? Because the passions of men will not conform to the dictates of reason and justice without constraint.

—Alexander Hamilton

If men were angels, no government would be necessary.

—James Madison

There can be no truer principle than this—that every individual of the community at large has an equal right to the protection of government.

—Alexander Hamilton

As Mankind becomes more liberal, they will be more apt to allow that all those who conduct themselves as worthy members of the community are equally entitled to the protections of civil government. I hope ever to see America among the foremost nations of justice and liberality.

—George Washington

The only proper functions of a government are: the police, to protect you from criminals; the army, to protect you from foreign invaders; and the courts, to protect your property and contracts from breach or fraud by others, and to settle disputes by rational rules, according to objective law.

—Ayn Rand

Everyone who receives the protection of society owes a return for the benefit.

—John Stuart Mill

It is not merely for today, but for all time to come that we should perpetuate for our children's children this great and free government, which we have enjoyed all our lives.

—Abraham Lincoln

Of course, the aim of a constitutional democracy is to safeguard the rights of the minority and avoid the tyranny of the majority.

—**Cornel West**

An oppressive government is more to be feared than a tiger.

—**Confucius**

Democracy is the worst form of Government except all those other forms that have been tried from time to time.

—**Winston Churchill**

We are so concerned to flatter the majority that we lose sight of how very often it is necessary, in order to preserve freedom for the minority, let alone for the individual, to face that majority down.

—**William F. Buckley, Jr.**

In a democracy, dissent is an act of faith.

—**J. William Fulbright**

The strongest democracies flourish from frequent and lively debate, but they endure when people of every background and belief find a way to set aside smaller differences in service of a greater purpose.

—**Barack Obama**

There are two things which will always be very difficult for a democratic nation: to start a war and to end it.

—Alexis de Tocqueville

❧

The spirit of democracy cannot be imposed from without. It has to come from within.

—Mahatma Gandhi

❧

A respect for the rights of other people to determine their forms of government and their economy will not weaken our democracy. It will inevitably strengthen it. One of the first things we must get rid of is the idea that democracy is tantamount to capitalism.

—Eleanor Roosevelt

❧

There cannot be true democracy unless women's voices are heard. There cannot be true democracy unless women are given the opportunity to take responsibility for their own lives. There cannot be true democracy unless all citizens are able to participate fully in the lives of their country.

—Hillary Clinton

❧

Societies held together by fear and repression may offer the illusion of stability for a time, but they are built upon fault lines that will eventually tear asunder.

—Barack Obama

Just because you do not take an interest in politics doesn't mean politics won't take an interest in you.

—**Pericles**

Man is by nature a political animal.

—**Aristotle**

Politics are such a torment that I would advise every one that I love not to mix with them.

—**Thomas Jefferson**

One of the penalties for refusing to participate in politics is that you end up being governed by your inferiors.

—**Plato**

I have nothing but contempt for the kind of governor who is afraid, for whatever reason, to follow the course that he knows is best for the State; and as for the man who sets private friendship above the public welfare—I have no use for him either.

—**Sophocles**

It takes a politician to run a government. A statesman is a politician who's been dead for fifteen years.

—**Harry S. Truman**

Truthfulness has never been counted among the political virtues, and lies have always been regarded as justifiable tools in political dealings.

—**Hannah Arendt**

Politics is perhaps the only profession for which no preparation is thought necessary.

—**Robert Louis Stevenson**

He knows nothing; and he thinks he knows everything. That points clearly to a political career.

—**George Bernard Shaw**

I have come to the conclusion that politics are too serious a matter to be left to the politicians.

—**Charles de Gaulle**

Politicians are the same all over. They promise to build a bridge even where there is no river.

—**Nikita Khrushchev**

Politics is far more complicated than physics.

—**Albert Einstein**

The modern conservative is engaged in one of man's oldest exercises in moral philosophy; that is, the search for a superior moral justification for selfishness.

—**John Kenneth Galbraith**

The truth is that all men having power ought to be mistrusted.

—**James Madison**

Mothers all want their sons to grow up to be president but they don't want them to become politicians in the process.

—**John F. Kennedy**

In war you can only be killed once, but in politics many times.

—**Winston Churchill**

Conservatives are not necessarily stupid, but most stupid people are conservatives.

—**John Stuart Mill**

One of the most pervasive political visions of our time is the vision of liberals as compassionate and conservatives as less caring.

—**Thomas Sowell**

PEACE AND WAR

The name of peace is sweet, and the thing itself is beneficial, but there is a great difference between peace and servitude. Peace is freedom in tranquility; servitude is the worst of all evils, to be resisted not only by war, but even by death.

—Cicero

❧

There is nothing so likely to produce peace as to be well prepared to meet an enemy.

—George Washington

❧

I believe that even amid today's mortar bursts and whining bullets, there is still hope for a brighter tomorrow. I believe that wounded justice, lying prostrate on the blood-flowing streets of our nations, can be lifted from this dust of shame to reign supreme among the children of men.

—Martin Luther King, Jr.

Peace is not unity in similarity but unity in diversity, in the comparison and conciliation of differences.

—**Mikhail Gorbachev**

You have to work with your enemy. Then he becomes your partner.

—**Nelson Mandela**

Especially now when views are becoming more polarized, we must work to understand each other across political, religious and national boundaries.

—**Jane Goodall**

We must learn to live together as brothers or perish together as fools.

—**Martin Luther King, Jr.**

Difference is of the essence of humanity. Difference is an accident of birth and it should therefore never be the source of hatred or conflict. The answer to difference is to respect it. Therein lies a most fundamental principle of peace: respect for diversity.

—**John Hume**

There has never been—there can never be—successful compromise between good and evil. Only total victory can reward the champions of tolerance and decency and freedom and faith.

—**Franklin D. Roosevelt**

Wars and revolutions and battles are due simply and solely to the body and its desires. All wars are undertaken for the acquisition of wealth; and the reason why we have to acquire wealth is the body, because we are slaves to its service.

—Socrates

When the rich make war, it is the poor who die.

—Jean-Paul Sartre

Wars shatter so many lives. I think especially of children robbed of their childhood.

—Pope Francis

Laws are silent in times of war.

—Cicero

Women have always been the primary victims of war. Women lose their husbands, their fathers, their sons in combat.

—Hillary Clinton

The more a country makes military weapons, the more insecure it becomes: if you have weapons, you become a target for attack.

—Albert Einstein

In such a world of conflict, a world of victims and executioners, it is the job of thinking people not to be on the side of the executioners.

—Albert Camus

Never, never, never believe any war will be smooth and easy, or that anyone who embarks on the strange voyage can measure the tides and hurricanes he will encounter. The statesman who yields to war fever must realize that once the signal is given, he is no longer the master of policy but the slave of unforeseeable and uncontrollable events.

—Winston Churchill

I have seen war. I have seen war on land and sea. I have seen blood running from the wounded. I have seen the dead in the mud. I have seen cities destroyed. I have seen children starving. I have seen the agony of mothers and wives. I hate war.

—Franklin D. Roosevelt

It has become appallingly obvious that our technology has exceeded our humanity.

—Albert Einstein

Mankind must put an end to war or war will put an end to mankind.

—John F. Kennedy

It is well that war is so terrible, or we should grow too fond of it.

—Robert E. Lee

∽

The peace we seek and need means much more than mere absence of war. It means the acceptance of law, and the fostering of justice, in all the world.

—Dwight D. Eisenhower

HISTORY

History is a guide to navigation in perilous times. History is who we are and why we are the way we are.

—David McCullough

History with its flickering lamp stumbles along the trail of the past, trying to reconstruct its scenes, to revive its echoes, and kindle with pale gleams the passion of former days.

—Winston Churchill

Even the most painstaking history is a bridge across an eternal mystery.

—Bruce Catton

Who does not know that the first law of historical writing is the truth.

—Cicero

History is not just about dates and quotations . . . It's about everything. It's about life history. It's human. And we have to see it that way. We have to teach it that way. We have to read it that way. It's about art, music, literature, money, science, love—the human experience.

—**David McCullough**

Very few things happen at the right time, and the rest do not happen at all; the conscientious historian will correct these defects.

—**Herodotus**

History is malleable. A new cache of diaries can shed new light, and archeological evidence can challenge our popular assumptions.

—**Ken Burns**

No great man lives in vain. The history of the world is but the biography of great men.

—**Thomas Carlyle**

Without words, without writing and without books there would be no history, there could be no concept of humanity.

—**Hermann Hesse**

The history of all hitherto existing society is the history of class struggles.

—**Karl Marx**

In books lies the soul of the whole Past Time; the articulate audible voice of the Past, when the body and material substance of it has altogether vanished like a dream.

—**Thomas Carlyle**

Books are the carriers of civilization. Without books, history is silent, literature dumb, science crippled, thought and speculation at a standstill.

—**Barbara Tuchman**

The whole history of the world is summed up in the fact that when nations are strong they are not always just, and when they wish to be just, they are often no longer strong.

—**Winston Churchill**

Human history becomes more and more a race between education and catastrophe.

—**H. G. Wells**

The causes of events are ever more interesting than the events themselves.

—**Cicero**

A nation that forgets its past can function no better than an individual with amnesia.

—**David McCullough**

I'm interested in the way in which the past affects the present and I think that if we understand a good deal more about history, we automatically understand a great more about contemporary life.

—Toni Morrison

Those who cannot remember the past are condemned to repeat it.

—George Santayana

Women have always been an equal part of the past. We just haven't been a part of history.

—Gloria Steinem

People are trapped in history, and history is trapped in them.

—James Baldwin

When great changes occur in history, when great principles are involved, as a rule the majority are wrong. The minority are right.

—Eugene V. Debs

All big changes in human history have been arrived at slowly and through many compromises.

—Eleanor Roosevelt

Neither a wise man or a brave man lies down on the tracks of history to wait for the train of the future to run over him.

—Dwight D. Eisenhower

If you want to understand today, you have to search yesterday.

—Pearl S. Buck

Once a president gets to the White House, the only audience that is left that really matters is history.

—Doris Kearns Goodwin

The drumbeat of history is quickening.

—Lyndon B. Johnson

History is filled with unforeseeable situations that call for some flexibility of action.

—Franklin D. Roosevelt

To be ignorant of what occurred before you were born is to remain forever a child.

—Cicero

A man who reviews the old so as to find out the new is qualified to teach others.

—**Confucius**

That men do not learn very much from the lessons of history is the most important of all the lessons that History has to teach.

—**Aldous Huxley**

History is more or less bunk. It's tradition. We don't want tradition. We want to live in the present and the only history that is worth a tinker's damn is the history we make today.

—**Henry Ford**

The main thing is to make history, not to write it.

—**Otto von Bismarck**

Mankind are so much the same, in all times and places, that history informs us of nothing new or strange in this particular. Its chief use is only to discover the constant and universal principles of human nature.

—**David Hume**

History, despite its wrenching pain, cannot be unlived, but if faced with courage, need not be lived again.

—**Maya Angelou**

ART, LITERATURE, AND MUSIC

Every man's work, whether it be literature, or music or pictures or architecture or anything else, is always a portrait of himself.

—Samuel Butler

All art is an imitation of nature.

—Seneca

Art washes away from the soul the dust of everyday life.

—Pablo Picasso

Every artist dips his brush in his own soul, and paints his own nature into his pictures.

—Henry Ward Beecher

Art should live in the heart of the people. Ordinary people should have the same ability to understand art as anybody else. I don't think art is elite or mysterious.

—Ai Weiwei

Artists do not experiment. Experiment is what scientists do; they initiate an operation of unknown factors to be instructed by its results. An artist puts down what he knows and at every moment it is what he knows at that moment.

—Gertrude Stein

Art is either plagiarism or revolution.

—Paul Gauguin

Painting is the grandchild of nature. It is related to God.

—Rembrandt

Every child is an artist. The problem is how to remain an artist once he grows up.

—Pablo Picasso

Whether you succeed or not is irrelevant, there is no such thing. Making your unknown known is the important thing.

—Georgia O'Keeffe

I paint my own reality. The only thing I know is that I paint because I need to, and I paint whatever passes through my head without any consideration.

—**Frida Kahlo**

Painting is silent poetry, and poetry is painting that speaks.

—**Plutarch**

If artists and poets are unhappy, it is after all because happiness does not interest them.

—**George Santayana**

One must work, nothing but work, and one must have patience.

—**Auguste Rodin**

I saw the angel in the marble and carved until I set him free.

—**Michelangelo**

My theory is that literature is essential to society in the way that dreams are essential to our lives. We can't live without dreaming—as we can't live without sleep. We are "conscious" beings for only a limited period of time, then we sink back into sleep—the "unconscious." It is nourishing, in ways we can't fully understand.

—**Joyce Carol Oates**

I cannot live without books.

—**Thomas Jefferson**

❧

The dearest ones of time, the strongest friends of the soul—BOOKS.

—**Emily Dickinson**

❧

Literature is my utopia.

—**Helen Keller**

❧

What matters in literature in the end is surely the idiosyncratic, the individual, the flavor or the color of a particular human suffering.

—**Harold Bloom**

❧

A book must be the ax for the frozen sea within us.

—**Franz Kafka**

❧

A writer—and, I believe, generally all persons—must think that whatever happens to him or her is a resource . . . All that happens to us, including our humiliations, our misfortunes, our embarrassments, all is given to us as raw material, as clay, so that we may shape our art.

—**Jorge Luis Borges**

Whatever I do is done out of sheer joy; I drop my fruits like a ripe tree. What the general reader or the critic makes of them is not my concern.

—**Henry Miller**

Writing has freed me from the despair of living.

—**Anita Brookner**

Medicine is my lawful wife. Literature is my mistress.

—**Anton Chekhov**

Nothing induces me to read a novel except when I have to make money by writing about it. I detest them.

—**Virginia Woolf**

The only sensible ends of literature are, first, the pleasurable toil of writing; second, the gratification of one's family and friends; and lastly, the solid cash.

—**Nathaniel Hawthorne**

We make out of the quarrel with others, rhetoric, but of the quarrel with ourselves, poetry.

—**William Butler Yeats**

Poetry, I have discovered, is always unexpected and always as faithful and honest as dreams.

—**Alice Walker**

Poetry is nearer to vital truth than history.

—**Plato**

Poetry is finer and more philosophical than history; for poetry expresses the universal, and history only the particular.

—**Aristotle**

Poetry is as exact a science as geometry.

—**Gustave Flaubert**

Music is a moral law. It gives soul to the universe, wings to the mind, flight to the imagination, and charm and gaiety to life and to everything.

—**Plato**

Who hears music, feels his solitude
Peopled at once

—**Robert Browning**

Beethoven can write music, thank God—but he can do nothing else on earth.

—**Ludwig van Beethoven**

∾

Mozart's music gives us permission to live.

—**John Updike**

∾

The genius of our country is improvisation, and jazz reflects that. It's our great contribution to the arts.

—**Ken Burns**

∾

A hundred years from now, people will listen to the music of the Beatles the same way we listen to Mozart.

—**Paul McCartney**

∾

In a world of peace and love, music would be the universal language.

—**Henry David Thoreau**

SCIENCE AND MATHEMATICS

Reason, observation, and experience—the Holy Trinity of Science.

—Robert G. Ingersoll

❧

Science is organized knowledge.

—Herbert Spencer

❧

Science is not only a disciple of reason but, also, one of romance and passion.

—Stephen Hawking

❧

A scientist in his laboratory is not a mere technician: he is also a child confronting natural phenomena that impress him as though they were fairy tales.

—Marie Curie

Science is not formal logic—it needs the free play of the mind in as great a degree as any other creative art. It is true that this is a gift which can hardly be taught, but its growth can be encouraged in those who already possess it.

—**Max Born**

❧

I like the scientific spirit—the holding off, the being sure but not too sure, the willingness to surrender ideas when the evidence is against them: this is ultimately fine—it always keeps the way beyond open.

—**Walt Whitman**

❧

Science does not know its debt to imagination.

—**Ralph Waldo Emerson**

❧

The great tragedy of Science—the slaying of a beautiful hypothesis by an ugly fact.

—**T. H. Huxley**

❧

In science, all facts, no matter how trivial or banal, enjoy democratic equality.

—**Mary McCarthy**

Science is what you know. Philosophy is what you don't know.

—Bertrand Russell

❧

Honorable errors do not count as failures in science, but as seeds for progress in the quintessential activity of correction.

—Stephen Jay Gould

❧

Sit down before fact as a little child, be prepared to give up every preconceived notion, follow humbly wherever and to whatever abyss nature leads, or you shall learn nothing.

—T. H. Huxley

❧

If I have seen farther than other men, it is because I stood on the shoulders of giants.

—Sir Isaac Newton

❧

By 2100, our destiny is to become like the gods we once worshipped and feared. But our tools will not be magic wands and potions but the science of computers, nanotechnology, artificial intelligence, biotechnology, and most of all, the quantum theory.

—Michio Kaku

❧

Pure mathematics is, in its way, the poetry of logical ideas.

—Albert Einstein

The laws of physics affect us all. Objective truths are true, whether or not you believe in them.

—Neil deGrasse Tyson

❧

Evolution is an inference from thousands of independent sources, the only conceptual structure that can make unified sense of all this disparate information.

—Stephen Jay Gould

❧

It may be bizarre, but in my opinion, science offers a sure path to God and religion.

—Paul Davies

❧

I do not feel obliged to believe that the same God who has endowed us with sense, reason, and intellect has intended us to forego their use.

—Galileo Galilei

❧

When I am in the company of scientists, I feel like a shabby curate who has strayed by mistake into a drawing room full of dukes.

—W. H. Auden

❧

Science may have found a cure for most evils; but it has found no remedy for the worst of them all—the apathy of human beings.

—Helen Keller

I am sorry to say there is too much point to the wise crack that life is extinct on other planets because their scientists were more advanced than ours.

—John F. Kennedy

~

Science can only ascertain what is, but not what should be, and outside of its domain value judgments of all kinds remain necessary.

—Albert Einstein

~

We especially need imagination in science. It is not all mathematics, nor all logic, but it is somewhat beauty and poetry.

—Maria Montessori

~

The mathematical sciences particularly exhibit order, symmetry, and limitation; and these are the greatest forms of the beautiful.

—Aristotle

~

Science literacy is the artery through which the solutions of tomorrow's problems flow.

—Neil deGrasse Tyson

~

Euclid taught me that without assumptions there is no proof. Therefore, in any argument, examine the assumptions.

—Eric Temple Bell

I often say that when you can measure what you are speaking about, and express it in numbers, you know something about it; but when you cannot measure it, when you cannot express it in numbers, your knowledge is of a meagre and unsatisfactory kind.

—**William Thomson, Lord Kelvin**

Let us grant that the pursuit of mathematics is a divine madness of the human spirit, a refuge from the goading urgency of contingent happenings.

—**Alfred North Whitehead**

I have hardly ever known a mathematician who was capable of reasoning.

—**Plato**

Nature is written in mathematical language.

—**Galileo Galilei**

Musical form is close to mathematics—not perhaps to mathematics itself, but certainly to something like mathematical thinking and relationship.

—**Igor Stravinsky**

Do not worry about your difficulties in mathematics. I can assure you mine are still greater.

—**Albert Einstein**

We can no more come to understand mathematics by examining its final product than we can understand the experience of music through simply looking at a score or an analysis of one; there is an experience that lies underneath and behind the systematic organization of the material.

—Edward Rothstein

Mathematics, rightly viewed, possesses not only truth, but supreme beauty—a beauty cold and austere, like that of sculpture.

—Bertrand Russell

HUMAN NATURE

Men go abroad to wonder at the height of mountains, at the huge waves of the sea, at the long courses of the rivers, at the vast compass of the ocean, at the circular motion of the stars, and they pass by themselves without wondering.

—St. Augustine

Morality, compassion, generosity are innate elements of the human constitution.

—Thomas Jefferson

Man is endowed by nature with organic relations to his fellow man; and natural impulse prompts him to consider the needs of others even when they compete with his own.

—Reinhold Niebuhr

It is while we are young that the habit of industry is formed. If not then, it never is afterwards. The fortune of our lives, therefore, depends on employing well the short period of youth.

—**Thomas Jefferson**

The tendency of man's nature to good is like the tendency of water to flow downward.

—**Mencius**

Human nature is potentially aggressive and destructive and potentially orderly and constructive.

—**Margaret Mead**

There are three classes of men; lovers of wisdom, lovers of honor, and lovers of gain.

—**Plato**

What passes as "human nature" is at most one-tenth nature, the other nine-tenths being nurture.

—**Bertrand Russell**

Great is the human who has not lost his childlike heart.

—**Mencius**

We agreed that ease in learning, a good memory, courage and high-mindedness belong to the philosophic nature.

—**Plato**

We are what we repeatedly do. Excellence, then, is not an act, but a habit.

—**Aristotle**

The human species is forever in a state of change, forever becoming.

—**Simone de Beauvoir**

I count him braver who conquers his desires than him who conquers his enemies; for the hardest victory is the victory over self.

—**Aristotle**

We are more often frightened than hurt; and we suffer more from imagination than from reality.

—**Seneca**

I learned that courage was not the absence of fear, but the triumph over it. The brave man is not he who does not feel afraid, but he who conquers that fear.

—**Nelson Mandela**

My greatest fear has always been that I would be afraid—afraid physically or mentally or morally and allow myself to be influenced by fear instead of by my honest convictions.

—**Eleanor Roosevelt**

The especial genius of women I believe to be electrical in movement, intuitive in function, spiritual in tendency.

—**Margaret Fuller**

Women deprived of the company of men pine, men deprived of the company of women become stupid.

—**Anton Chekhov**

Wise men speak because they have something to say; fools because they have to say something.

—**Plato**

Such is the nature of men, that howsoever they may acknowledge many others to be more witty, or more eloquent, or more learned; yet they will hardly believe there be many so wise as themselves.

—**Thomas Hobbes**

I love mankind—it's people I can't stand.

—**Charles M. Schulz,** *Peanuts*

You know what charm is: a way of getting the answer yes without having asked any clear question.

—**Albert Camus**

❧

A pessimist is one who makes difficulties of his opportunities and an optimist is one who makes opportunities of his difficulties.

—**Harry S. Truman**

❧

Everything that irritates us about others can lead us to an understanding of ourselves.

—**Carl Jung**

❧

Nobody realizes that some people expend tremendous energy merely to be normal.

—**Albert Camus**

❧

The whole problem with the world is that fools and fanatics are always so certain of themselves, and wiser people so full of doubts.

—**Bertrand Russell**

❧

What is tolerance? It is the consequence of humanity. We are all formed of frailty and error; let us pardon reciprocally each other's folly—that is the first law of nature.

—**Voltaire**

Tolerance and compassion are active, not passive states, born of the capacity to listen, to observe and to respect others.

—**Indira Gandhi**

When people die, they cannot be replaced. They leave holes that cannot be filled, for it is the fate—the genetic and neural fate—of every human being to be a unique individual, to find his own path, to live his own life, to die his own death.

—**Oliver Sacks**

The spirit is the true self.

—**Cicero**

If we are to achieve a richer culture, rich in contrasting values, we must recognize the whole gamut of human potentialities, and so weave a less arbitrary social fabric, one in which each diverse human gift will find a fitting place.

—**Margaret Mead**

I refuse to allow any man-made differences to separate me from any other human beings.

—**Maya Angelou**

We are all different, but we share the same human spirit. Perhaps it's human nature that we adapt and survive.

—Stephen Hawking

We become not a melting pot but a beautiful mosaic. Different people, different beliefs, different yearnings, different hopes, different dreams.

—Jimmy Carter

My humanity is bound up in yours, for we can only be human together.

—Desmond Tutu

If I seem to boast more than is becoming, my excuse is that I brag for humanity rather than for myself.

—Henry David Thoreau

HAPPINESS

Most folks are about as happy as they make up their minds to be.

—**Abraham Lincoln**

Happiness depends more upon the internal frame of a person's own mind, than on the externals in the world.

—**George Washington**

It is neither wealth nor splendor, but tranquility and occupation, which give happiness.

—**Thomas Jefferson**

Happiness is when what you think, what you say, and what you do are in harmony.

—**Mahatma Gandhi**

There is only one happiness in life, to love and be loved.

—George Sand

❧

Happiness is determined by factors like your health, your family relationships and friendships, and above all by feeling that you are in control of how you spend your time.

—Daniel Kahneman

❧

The man is to be envied who has been fortunate in his children, and has avoided dire calamity.

—Euripides

❧

Grief can take care of itself; but to get the full value of a joy you must have somebody to divide it with.

—Mark Twain

❧

He is happiest, be he king or peasant, who finds peace in his home.

—Goethe

❧

Many persons have a wrong idea of what constitutes true happiness. It is not attained through self-gratification but through fidelity to a worthy purpose.

—Helen Keller

That is happiness: to be dissolved into something complete and great.

—Willa Cather

Those who are happiest are those who do the most for others.

—Booker T. Washington

Happiness is neither virtue nor pleasure nor this thing nor that but simply growth. We are happy when we are growing.

—William Butler Yeats

But I don't think of the future, or the past, I feast on the moment. This is the secret of happiness, but only reached now in middle age.

—Virginia Woolf

Just as a cautious businessman avoids investing all his capital in one concern, so wisdom would probably admonish us also not to anticipate all our happiness from one quarter alone.

—Sigmund Freud

Man is fond of counting his troubles, but he does not count his joys. If he counted them up as he ought to, he would see that every lot has enough happiness provided for it.

—Fyodor Dostoevsky

Whether happiness may come or not, one should try and prepare one's self to do without it.

—George Eliot

∾

You will never be happy if you continue to search for what happiness consists of. You will never live if you are looking for the meaning of life.

—Albert Camus

∾

Ask yourself whether you are happy, and you cease to be so.

—John Stuart Mill

∾

Silence. All human unhappiness comes from not knowing how to stay quietly in a room.

—Blaise Pascal

∾

A sound mind in a sound body, is a short, but full description of a happy state in this World: he that has these two, has little more to wish for; and he that wants either of them, will be little the better for anything else.

—John Locke

Happiness is not a matter of intensity but of balance, order, rhythm and harmony.

—**Thomas Merton**

Human felicity is produced not so much by great pieces of good fortune that seldom happen, as by little advantages that occur every day.

—**Benjamin Franklin**

RELIGION, MORALITY, AND VIRTUE

That is the religious experience: the astonishment of meeting someone who is waiting for you.

—Pope Francis

∽

I believe in order to understand.

—St. Augustine

∽

Despite theological differences, all great religions share common commitments that define our ideal secular relationships. I am convinced that Christians, Buddhists, Jews, and others can embrace each other in a common effort to alleviate human suffering and to espouse peace.

—Jimmy Carter

It is this belief in a power larger than myself and other than myself which allows me to venture into the unknown and even the unknowable.

—**Maya Angelou**

Ah, *mon cher*, for anyone who is alone, without God and without a master, the weight of days is dreadful.

—**Albert Camus, *The Fall***

I gave in, and admitted that God was God.

—**C. S. Lewis**

Belief consists in accepting the affirmations of the soul; unbelief, in denying them.

—**Ralph Waldo Emerson**

To one who has faith, no explanation is necessary. To one without faith, no explanation is possible.

—**St. Thomas Aquinas**

I have read in Plato and Cicero sayings that are wise and very beautiful; but I have never read in either of them: Come unto me all ye that labor and are heavy laden.

—**St. Augustine**

The cross symbolizes a cosmic as well as historic truth. Love conquers the world, but its victory is not an easy one.

—**Reinhold Niebuhr**

Religion is to do right. It is to love, it is to serve, it is to think, it is to be humble.

—**Ralph Waldo Emerson**

This is my simple religion. There is no need for temples; no need for complicated philosophy. Our own brain, our own heart is our temple; the philosophy is kindness.

—**Dalai Lama**

Whatever your heart clings to and confides in, that is really your God.

—**Martin Luther**

My religion is nature. That's what arouses those feelings of wonder and mysticism and gratitude in me.

—**Oliver Sacks**

Not only are we in the universe, the universe is in us. I don't know of any deeper spiritual feeling than what that brings upon me.

—**Neil deGrasse Tyson**

My country is the world, and my religion is to do good.

—**Thomas Paine**

I happen to be a Christian, but I know that there is one God. People worshipping goodness and love and kindness and truth are worshipping the same God.

—**Anne Lamott**

There is no higher religion than human service. To work for the common good is the highest creed.

—**Albert Schweitzer**

I really only love God as much as I love the person I love the least.

—**Dorothy Day**

All the religions of the world, while they may differ in other respects, unitedly proclaim that nothing lives in this world but Truth.

—**Mahatma Gandhi**

It is the repeated performance of just and temperate actions that produces virtue.

—**Aristotle**

Preachers err by trying to talk people into belief; better they reveal the radiance of their own discovery.

—Joseph Campbell

It is of the essence of virtue that the good is not to be done for the sake of a reward.

—Abraham Joshua Heschel

The law that is within us we call conscience.

—Immanuel Kant

Whatever the source of moral knowledge might be—divine commandments or moral reason—every sane man, it was assumed, carried within himself a voice that tells him what is right and what is wrong, and this regardless of the law of the land and regardless of the voices of his fellowmen.

—Hannah Arendt

Courage is more exhilarating than fear and in the long run it is easier. We do not have to become heroes overnight. Just a step at a time, meeting each thing that comes up, seeing it is not as dreadful as it appeared, discovering we have the strength to stare it down.

—Eleanor Roosevelt

To know what is right and not to do it is the worst cowardice.

—Confucius

❧

Virtue is herself her own coveted reward.

—Ovid

❧

I like the silent church before the service begins, better than any preaching.

—Ralph Waldo Emerson

❧

Character cannot be developed in ease and quiet. Only through experience of trial and suffering can the soul be strengthened, ambition inspired, and success achieved.

—Helen Keller

❧

Humility is the foundation of all the other virtues hence, in the soul in which this virtue does not exist there cannot be any other virtue except in mere appearance.

—St. Augustine

❧

Try not to become a person of success, but rather try to become a person of value.

—Albert Einstein

Virtue comes to the virtuous by the gift of God.

—Socrates

Character is simply habit long enough continued.

—Plutarch

Courage is resistance to fear, mastery of fear, not absence of fear.

—Mark Twain

Economy, prudence, and a simple life are the sure masters of need, and will often accomplish that which, their opposites, with a fortune at hand, will fail to do.

—Clara Barton

Humility must always be the portion of any man who receives acclaim earned in blood of his followers and sacrifices of his friends.

—Dwight D. Eisenhower

Nothing comes of so many things, if you have patience.

—Joyce Carol Oates

Vice is waste of life.

—George Bernard Shaw

We only excite envy in a child by telling him to compare his own worth with the worth of others.

—**Immanuel Kant**

A simple lifestyle is good for us, helping us to better share with those in need.

—**Pope Francis**

We must be as courteous to a man as we are to a picture, which we are willing to give the advantage of a good light.

—**Ralph Waldo Emerson**

The true measure of a man is how he treats someone who can do him absolutely no good.

—**Samuel Johnson**

Have patience with all things, but first of all with yourself.

—**St. Francis de Sales**

The strength of a man's virtue must not be measured by his efforts, but by his ordinary life.

—**Blaise Pascal**

Circumstances are beyond human control, but our conduct is in our own power.

—**Benjamin Disraeli**

A word once let out of the cage cannot be whistled back again.

—**Horace**

The chains of habit are too weak to be felt until they are too strong to be broken.

—**Samuel Johnson**

The simplest and shortest ethical precept is to be served by others as little as possible, and to serve others as much as possible.

—**Leo Tolstoy**

It has ever been my experience that folks who have no vices have very few virtues.

—**Abraham Lincoln**

Gentleness, self-sacrifice and generosity are the exclusive possession of no one race or religion.

—**Mahatma Gandhi**

The less a man thinks or knows about his virtues, the better we like him.

—**Ralph Waldo Emerson**

Wisdom, compassion, and courage are the three universally recognized moral qualities of men.

—**Confucius**

It is by doing good that we become good.

—**Jean-Jacques Rousseau**

In spite of everything, I still believe that people are really good at heart.

—**Anne Frank**

WEALTH AND POVERTY

No man is born rich. Every man, when he first sees light, is commanded to be content with milk and rags. Such is our beginning, and yet kingdoms are all too small for us!

— Seneca

The life of money-making is one undertaken under compulsion, and wealth is evidently not the good we are seeking; for it is merely useful and for the sake of something else.

— Aristotle

I don't believe in a law to prevent a man from getting rich; it would do more harm than good. So while we do not propose any war upon capital, we do wish to allow the humblest man an equal chance to get rich with everybody else.

— Abraham Lincoln

The greatest wealth is a poverty of desires.

—Seneca

Money is the root of all evil, and yet it is such a useful root that we cannot go on without it any more than we can without potatoes.

—Louisa May Alcott

Money has never made man happy, nor will it, there is nothing in its nature to produce happiness. The more of it one has the more one wants.

—Benjamin Franklin

Any fool can spend money. But to earn it and save it and defer gratification—then you learn to value it differently.

—Malcolm Gladwell

An imbalance between rich and poor is the oldest and most fatal ailment of all republics.

—Plato

Money has no utility to me beyond a certain point. Its utility is entirely in building an organization and getting the resources out to the poorest in the world.

—Bill Gates

Being the richest man in the cemetery doesn't matter to me. Going to bed at night saying we've done something wonderful, that's what matters to me.

—Steve Jobs

Piling up material goods cannot fill the emptiness of lives which have no confidence or purpose.

—Jimmy Carter

Most of the luxuries and many of the so-called comforts of life are not only not indispensable, but positive hindrances to the elevation of mankind.

—Henry David Thoreau

A scholar who cherishes the love of comfort is not fit to be deemed a scholar.

—Lao Tzu

Money makes a good servant, but a bad master.

—Francis Bacon

Remember that time is money.

—Benjamin Franklin

It is more rewarding to watch money change the world than watch it accumulate.

—Gloria Steinem

It is preoccupation with possessions, more than anything else that prevents us from living freely and nobly.

—Bertrand Russell

What's money? A man is a success if he gets up in the morning and goes to bed at night and in between does what he wants to do.

—Bob Dylan

There are only two families in the world, as a grandmother of mine used to say: the haves and the have-nots.

—Cervantes, *Don Quixote*

Money, it turned out, was exactly like sex, you thought of nothing else if you didn't have it and thought of other things if you did.

—James Baldwin

The fight against poverty and hunger must be fought constantly and on many fronts, especially in its causes.

—Pope Francis

Can anybody remember when the times were not hard, and money not scarce?

—**Ralph Waldo Emerson**

Anyone who has ever struggled with poverty knows how extremely expensive it is to be poor.

—**James Baldwin**

I find that principles have no real force except when one is well fed.

—**Mark Twain**

The only way not to think of money is to have a great deal of it.

—**Edith Wharton**

Loneliness and the feeling of being unwanted is the most terrible poverty.

—**Mother Teresa**

Poor is not the person who has too little, but the person who craves more.

—**Seneca**

Give me the poverty that enjoys true wealth.

—**Henry David Thoreau**

LIFE'S PLEASURES

The happiest moments of my life have been the few which I have passed at home in the bosom of my family.

—Thomas Jefferson

❧

For what should a man live, if not for the pleasures of discourse?

—Plato

❧

After all, the only proper intoxication is conversation.

—Oscar Wilde

❧

I am never long, even in the society of her I love, without yearning for the company of my lamp and my library.

—Lord Byron

The human frame being what it is, heart, body and brain all mixed together, and not contained in separate compartments as they will be no doubt in another million years, a good dinner is of great importance to good talk. One cannot think well, love well, sleep well, if one has not dined well.

—Virginia Woolf

There are perhaps no days of our childhood we lived so fully as those we spent with a favorite book.

—Marcel Proust

How many a man has dated a new era in his life from the reading of a book! The book exists for us, perchance, that will explain our miracles and reveal new ones. The at present unutterable things we may find somewhere uttered.

—Henry David Thoreau

I have given up newspapers in exchange for Tacitus and Thucydides, for Newton and Euclid; and I find myself much the happier.

—Thomas Jefferson

A room without books is like a body without a soul.

—Cicero

A home is no home unless it contain food and fire for the mind as well as for the body. . . . For human beings are not so constituted that they can live without expansion. If they do not get it in one way, they must another, or perish.

—Margaret Fuller

I always turn to the sports pages first, which records people's accomplishments. The front page has nothing but man's failures.

—Earl Warren

I soon experienced a real pleasure in the task of writing, and the three or four hours in the middle of every day, often devoted to slumber or cards, saw me industriously at work.

—Winston Churchill

Every now and then go away, have a little relaxation, for when you come back to your work your judgment will be surer. Go some distance away because then the work appears smaller and more of it can be taken in at a glance and a lack of harmony and proportion is more readily seen.

—Leonardo da Vinci

Without work, all life goes rotten, but when work is soulless, life stifles and dies.

—Albert Camus

I cannot face with comfort the idea of life without work; work and the free play of the imagination are for me the same thing, I take no pleasure in anything else.

—Sigmund Freud

Play should never be allowed to interfere with work; and a life devoted merely to play is, of all forms of existence, the most dismal.

—Theodore Roosevelt

I think I should have no other mortal wants, if I could always have plenty of music. It seems to infuse strength into my limbs, and ideas into my brain. Life seems to go on without effort, when I am filled with music.

—George Eliot

But nothing is so damaging to good character as the habit of lounging at the games; for then it is that vice steals subtly upon one through the avenue of pleasure.

—Seneca

I could not live without champagne. In victory I deserve it. In defeat I need it.

—Winston Churchill

Wine makes a man more pleased with himself; I do not say that it makes him more pleasing to others.

—Samuel Johnson

Good wine is a necessity of life for me.

—Thomas Jefferson

No form of art goes beyond ordinary consciousness as film does, straight to our emotions, deep into the twilight room of the soul.

—Ingmar Bergman

Our emotions rise to meet the force coming from the screen, and they go on rising throughout our movie-going lives.

—Pauline Kael

The theater is so endlessly fascinating because it's so accidental. It's so much like life.

—Arthur Miller

One of the blessings of life in the rural areas is the fact that any child or adult can escape and be alone with nature at a moment's notice.

—Eleanor Roosevelt

Many men go fishing all of their lives without knowing that it is not fish they are after.

—Henry David Thoreau

The game of baseball has always been linked in my mind with the mystic texture of childhood, with the sounds and smells of summer nights, and with the memories of my father.

—Doris Kearns Goodwin

Animals are such agreeable friends—they ask no questions, they pass no criticisms.

—George Eliot

The great pleasure of a dog is that you may make a fool of yourself with him and not only will he not scold you, but he will make a fool of himself too.

—Samuel Butler

The less we indulge our pleasures the more we enjoy them.

—Juvenal

If one oversteps the bounds of moderation, the greatest pleasures cease to please.

—Epictetus

As much as I converse with sages and heroes, they have very little of my love or admiration. I long for rural and domestic scenes, for the warbling of birds and the prattle of my children.

—**John Adams**

Tranquility is the old man's milk. I go to enjoy it in a few days, and to exchange the roar and tumult of bulls and bears for the prattle of my grandchildren and senile rest.

—**Thomas Jefferson**

HARDSHIP, ADVERSITY, AND HOPE

The beginning of hardship is like the first taste of bitter food—it seems for a moment unbearable; yet, if there is nothing else to satisfy our hunger, we take another bite and find it possible to go on.

—George Eliot

Most men ebb and flow in wretchedness between the fear of death and the hardship of life; they are unwilling to live, and yet they do not know how to die.

—Seneca

In this sad world of ours, sorrow comes to all; and, to the young, it comes with bitterest agony, because it takes them unawares.

—Abraham Lincoln

There is no education like adversity.

—Benjamin Disraeli

No untroubled day has ever dawned for me.

—Seneca

Nothing is more desirable than to be released from an affliction, but nothing is more frightening than to be divested of a crutch.

—James Baldwin

If life becomes hard to bear we think of a change in our circumstances. But the most important and effective change, a change in our own attitude, hardly even occurs to us.

—Ludwig Wittgenstein

Your life is not going to be easy, and it should not be easy. It ought to be hard. It ought to be radical; it ought to be restless; it ought to lead you to places you'd rather not go.

—Henri Nouwen

In so far as the mind is stronger than the body, so are the ills contracted by the mind more severe than those contracted by the body.

—Cicero

The mind is still haunted with its old unconscious ways; it broods on lost authorities; and the yearning, the deep and hollowing yearning for divine volition and service is with us still.

—Julian Jaynes

The keenest sorrow is to recognize ourselves as the sole cause of all our adversities.

—Sophocles

The mass of men lead lives of quiet desperation.

—Henry David Thoreau

The thing of it is, we must live with the living.

—Montaigne

Everybody has losses—it's unavoidable in life. Sharing our pain is very healing.

—Isabel Allende

Let me embrace thee, sour adversity, for wise men say it is the wisest course.

—William Shakespeare

You may encounter many defeats, but you must not be defeated. In fact, it may be necessary to encounter the defeats, so you can know who you are, what you can rise from, how you can still come out of it.

—**Maya Angelou**

Self-pity is our worst enemy and if we yield to it, we can never do anything wise in this world.

—**Helen Keller**

Don't go around saying the world owes you a living. The world owes you nothing. It was here first.

—**Mark Twain**

Man needs difficulties; they are necessary for health.

—**Carl Jung**

To search for power within myself means I must be willing to move through being afraid to whatever lies beyond.

—**Audre Lorde**

Only the dead have seen the end of the war.

—**Plato**

Part of being optimistic is keeping one's head pointed toward the sun, one's feet moving forward. There were many dark moments when my faith in humanity was sorely tested, but I would not and could not give myself up to despair. That way lays defeat and death.

—Nelson Mandela

❧

I am not afraid of storms for I am learning how to sail my ship.

—Louisa May Alcott

❧

We could never learn to be brave and patient, if there were only joy in the world.

—Helen Keller

❧

The ultimate measure of a man is not where he stands in moments of comfort and convenience, but where he stands at times of challenge and controversy.

—Martin Luther King, Jr.

❧

Even a happy life cannot be without a measure of darkness, and the word "happy" would lose its meaning if it were not balanced by sadness.

—Carl Jung

The measure of success is not whether you have a tough problem to deal with, but whether it's the same problem you had last year.

—**John Foster Dulles**

After climbing a great hill, one only finds that there are many more hills to climb.

—**Nelson Mandela**

Prosperity is not without many fears and disasters; and adversity is not without comforts and hopes.

—**Francis Bacon**

It is from pain and our own limits where we best learn to grow, and from our own flaws surges the deep question: haven't we suffered enough to decide to break old patterns?

—**Pope Francis**

Those who have never despaired have neither lived nor loved. Hope is inseparable from despair. Those of us who truly hope make despair a constant companion whom we out-wrestle every day owing to our commitment to justice, love, and hope.

—**Cornel West**

We must accept our pain, change what we can, and laugh at the rest.

—Camille Paglia

Just as despair can come to one only from other human beings, hope, too, can be given to one only by other human beings.

—Elie Wiesel

Hope is itself a species of happiness, and, perhaps, the chief happiness which this world affords.

—Samuel Johnson

THE WORLD AROUND US

To put the world right in order, we must first put the nation in order;
to put the nation in order, we must first put the family in order; to put
the family in order, we must first cultivate our personal life; we must
first set our hearts right.

—Confucius

❧

The world is a dangerous place; not because of those who do evil, but
because of those who look on and do nothing.

—Albert Einstein

❧

The world is very different now. For man holds in his mortal hands
the power to abolish all forms of human poverty, and all forms of
human life.

—John F. Kennedy

Wherever men and women are persecuted because of their race, religion, or political views, that place must—at that moment— become the center of the universe.

—Elie Wiesel

There is a sufficiency in the world for man's need but not for man's greed.

—Mahatma Gandhi

Never doubt that a small group of thoughtful committed citizens can change the world. In fact, it's the only thing that ever has.

—Margaret Mead

Yours is not the task of making your way in the world, but the task of remaking the world which you will find before you.

—Franklin D. Roosevelt

The first resistance to social change is to say it's not necessary.

—Gloria Steinem

What sets worlds in motion is the interplay of differences, their attractions and repulsions. Life is plurality, death is uniformity. By suppressing differences and peculiarities, by eliminating different civilizations and cultures, progress weakens life and favors death.

—Octavio Paz

What's the use of a fine house if you haven't got a tolerable planet to put it on?

—Henry David Thoreau

❧

We won't have a society if we destroy the environment.

—Margaret Mead

❧

The world has changed far more in the past 100 years than in any other century in history. The reason is not political or economic but technological—technologies that flowed directly from advances in basic science.

—Stephen Hawking

❧

It may be the business of great thinkers to unmask the world and despise it. But to me only one thing is important: the ability to love the world, to contemplate it and myself and all other beings with love and wonder and veneration.

—Hermann Hesse

❧

The earth will not continue to offer its harvest, except with faithful stewardship. We cannot say we love the land and then take steps to destroy it for use by future generations.

—Pope John Paul II

It is horrifying that we have to fight our own government to save the environment.

—**Ansel Adams**

❧

You see things; and you say, "Why?" But I dream things that never were; and I say, "Why not?"

—**George Bernard Shaw**

❧

This world is but a canvas to our imagination.

—**Henry David Thoreau**

❧

Change will not come if we wait for some other person or some other time. We are the ones we've been waiting for. We are the change that we seek.

—**Barack Obama**

❧

None of us alone can save the nation or the world. But each of us can make a positive difference if we commit ourselves to do so.

—**Cornel West**

❧

I alone cannot change the world, but I can cast a stone across the waters to create many ripples.

—**Mother Teresa**

Each of us must rededicate ourselves to serving the common good. We are a community. Our individual Fates are linked; our futures intertwined; and if we act in that knowledge and in that spirit together, as the Bible says: "We can move mountains."

—**Jimmy Carter**

The golden way is to be friends with the world and to regard the whole human family as one.

—**Mahatma Gandhi**

WIT AND WISDOM

Wit is educated insolence.

—**Aristotle**

✺

There is nothing so absurd but some philosopher has said it.

—**Cicero**

✺

Those people who think they know everything are a great annoyance to those of us who do.

—**Isaac Asimov**

✺

Men do not care how nobly they live, but only how long, although it is within the reach of every man to live nobly, but within no man's power to live long.

—**Seneca**

Better to remain silent and be thought a fool than to speak out and remove all doubt.

—**Abraham Lincoln**

If two men agree on everything, you may be sure that one of them is doing the thinking.

—**Lyndon B. Johnson**

Life is like a bicycle. To keep your balance, you must keep moving.

—**Albert Einstein**

Wisdom doesn't necessarily come with age. Sometimes age just shows up all by itself.

—**Woodrow Wilson**

True wisdom comes to each of us when we realize how little we understand about life, ourselves, and the world around us.

—**Socrates**

I'm astounded by people who want to "know" the universe when it's hard enough to find your way around Chinatown.

—**Woody Allen**

Life brings sorrows and joys alike. It is what a man does with them—not what they do to him—that is the true test of his mettle.

—**Theodore Roosevelt**

Life is never easy. There is work to be done and obligations to be met—obligations to truth, to justice, and to liberty.

—**John F. Kennedy**

Life appears to me too short to be spent in nursing animosity or registering wrongs.

—**Charlotte Brontë**

He can compress the most words into the smallest idea of any man I ever met.

—**Abraham Lincoln**

Life is what happens to you when you're busy making other plans.

—**John Lennon**

There is more to life than increasing its speed.

—**Mahatma Gandhi**

I never submitted the whole system of my opinions to the creed of any party of men whatever, in religion, in philosophy, in politics or in anything else, where I was capable of thinking for myself. Such an addiction is the last degradation of a free and moral agent. If I could not go to Heaven but with a party, I would not go there at all.

—**Thomas Jefferson**

Life was meant to be lived, and curiosity must be kept alive. One must never, for whatever reason, turn his back on life.

—**Eleanor Roosevelt**

Life is the sum of all your choices.

—**Albert Camus**

Nothing in life is to be feared, it is only to be understood. Now is the time to understand more, so that we may fear less.

—**Marie Curie**

To find yourself, think for yourself.

—**Socrates**

Think wrongly, if you please, but in all cases think for yourself.

—**Doris Lessing**

Nothing is at last sacred but the integrity of our own mind.

—**Ralph Waldo Emerson**

༄

The unexamined life is not worth living.

—**Socrates**

༄

He is a wise man who does not grieve for the things which he has not, but rejoices for those which he has.

—**Epictetus**

༄

You have to trust in something—your gut, destiny, life, karma, whatever. This approach has never let me down, and it has made all the difference in my life.

—**Steve Jobs**

༄

If a man does not keep pace with his companions, perhaps it is because he hears a different drummer. Let him step to the music which he hears, however measured or far away.

—**Henry David Thoreau**

༄

It is happier to be sometimes cheated than not to trust.

—**Samuel Johnson**

Make yourself necessary to someone.

—Ralph Waldo Emerson

Love all, trust a few, do wrong to none.

—William Shakespeare

Keep away from people who try to belittle your ambitions. Small people always do that, but the really great make you feel that you, too, can become great.

—Mark Twain

Associate yourself with people of good quality, for it is better to be alone than in bad company.

—Booker T. Washington

Make it a point to do something every day that you don't want to do. This is the golden rule for acquiring the habit of doing your duty without pain.

—Mark Twain

If you pursue evil with pleasure, the pleasure passes away and the evil remains; if you pursue good with labor, the labor passes away but the good remains.

—Cicero

No man chooses evil because it is evil; he only mistakes it for happiness, the good he seeks.

—**Mary Wollstonecraft**

Success is a lousy teacher. It seduces smart people into thinking they can't lose.

—**Bill Gates**

In three words I can sum up everything I've learned about life: it goes on.

—**Robert Frost**

My great concern is not whether you have failed, but whether you are content with failure.

—**Abraham Lincoln**

No man steps in the same river twice, for it is not the same river and he is not the same man.

—**Heraclitus**

The values of the world we inhabit and the people we surround ourselves with have a profound effect on who we are.

—**Malcolm Gladwell**

Really pay attention to negative feedback and solicit it, particularly from friends. . . . Hardly anyone does that, and it's incredibly helpful.

—Elon Musk

❧

In matters of style, swim with the current; in matters of principle, stand like a rock.

—Thomas Jefferson

❧

Familiarity breeds contempt, but it also breeds something like affection. We get used to the chains we wear, and we miss them when removed.

—John Dewey

❧

Cautious, careful people, always casting about to preserve their reputation and social standing, never can bring about a reform. Those who are really in earnest must be willing to be anything or nothing in the world's estimation.

—Susan B. Anthony

❧

Deal with yourself as an individual worthy of respect, and make everyone else deal with you the same way.

—Nikki Giovanni

Whether you think that you can or you can't, you're usually right.

—Henry Ford

When people show you who they are, believe them.

—Maya Angelou

Be content with what you have; rejoice in the way things are. When you realize there is nothing lacking, the whole world belongs to you.

—Lao Tzu

What you leave behind is not what is engraved in stone monuments, but what is woven into the lives of others.

—Pericles

To err is human; to forgive, divine.

—Alexander Pope

The afternoon of human life must also have a significance of its own and cannot be merely a pitiful appendage to life's morning.

—Carl Jung

Take care of this moment.

—**Mahatma Gandhi**

Nothing is worth more than this day.

—**Goethe**

Do not lose your enthusiasm. In its Greek etymology, the word *enthusiasm* means "God in us."

—**Ken Burns**

The miracle is that we are here, that no matter how undone we've been the night before, we wake up every morning and are still here. It is phenomenal just to be.

—**Anne Lamott**

The whole life of a man is but a point in time; let us enjoy it.

—**Plutarch**

Drop the question what tomorrow may bring, and count as profit every day that fate allows you.

—**Horace**

Love and work are the cornerstones of our humanness.

—Sigmund Freud

If you have built castles in the air, your work need not be lost; that is where they should be. Now put the foundations under them.

—Henry David Thoreau

Make the best use of what's in your power and take the rest as it happens.

—Epictetus

We're so engaged in doing things to achieve purposes of outer value that we forget the inner value, the rapture that is associated with being alive, is what it is all about.

—Joseph Campbell

However bad life may seem, there is always something you can do, and succeed at. While there's life, there is hope.

—Stephen Hawking

CONTRIBUTORS

Abigail Adams *(1744–1818)* — American writer and wife of John Adams

Ansel Adams *(1902–1984)* — American photographer and environmentalist

John Adams *(1735–1826)* — 2nd President of the United States

Louisa May Alcott *(1832–1888)* — American novelist

Woody Allen *(b. 1935)* — American actor, writer, director, comedian, and playwright

Isabel Allende *(b. 1942)* — Chilean-American writer

Marian Anderson *(1897–1993)* — American opera singer and activist

Maya Angelou *(1928–2014)* — American writer, poet, and civil rights activist

Susan B. Anthony *(1820–1906)* — American activist and key figure in the U.S. women's rights movement

St. Thomas Aquinas *(c. 1225–1274)* — Italian Dominican friar, priest, philosopher, theologian, and Doctor of the Church

Hannah Arendt *(1906–1975)* — German-born American political philosopher

Aristophanes *(c. 446–c. 386 B.C.)* — Greek dramatist

Aristotle *(384–322 B.C.)* — Greek philosopher

Isaac Asimov *(1920–1992)* — Russian-born American writer and biochemist

W. H. Auden *(1907–1973)* — English-born American poet and playwright

St. Augustine *(354–430)* — African-born Bishop and Doctor of the Church

Jane Austen *(1775–1817)* — English novelist

Francis Bacon *(1561–1626)* — English philosopher, scientist, orator, and author

James Baldwin *(1924–1987)* — American writer and activist

Clara Barton *(1821–1912)* — American nurse and founder of the American Red Cross

Henry Ward Beecher *(1813–1887)* — American clergyman and social reformer

Ludwig van Beethoven *(1770–1827)* — German composer and pianist

Eric Temple Bell *(1883–1960)* — Scottish-born mathematician and writer

Ingmar Bergman *(1918–2007)* — Swedish director, writer, and producer

Harold Bloom *(b. 1930)* — American writer, literary critic, and academic

Jorge Luis Borges *(1899–1986)* — Argentine writer, editor, and critic

Max Born *(1882–1970)* — German physicist and mathematician

Louis D. Brandeis *(1856–1941)* — American jurist

Charlotte Brontë *(1816–1855)* — English novelist and poet

Anita Brookner *(1928–2016)* — British novelist and art historian

Robert Browning *(1812–1889)* — English poet and playwright

Pearl S. Buck *(1892–1973)* — American novelist

William F. Buckley, Jr. *(1925–2008)* — American writer and political commentator

Edmund Burke *(1729–1797)* — Irish philosopher and statesman

Ken Burns *(b. 1953)* — American filmmaker

Leo Buscaglia *(1924–1998)* — American motivational speaker, writer, and professor

Samuel Butler *(1835–1902)* — British novelist and essayist

Lord Byron *(1788–1824)* — English poet

Julius Caesar *(100–44 b.c.)* — Roman general and statesman

Joseph Campbell *(1904–1987)* — American mythologist, writer, and lecturer

Albert Camus *(1913–1960)* — French novelist, essayist, and dramatist

Thomas Carlyle *(1795–1881)* — Scottish historian and political philosopher

Jimmy Carter *(b. 1924)* — 39th President of the United States and human rights advocate

George Washington Carver *(c. 1864–1943)* — American scientist, educator, and inventor

Willa Cather *(1873–1947)* — American novelist

Carrie Chapman Catt *(1859–1947)* — American suffrage leader

Bruce Catton *(1899–1978)* — American historian and journalist

Cervantes (Miguel de Cervantes Saavedra) *(1547–1616)* — Spanish novelist and dramatist

Anton Chekhov *(1860–1904)* — Russian dramatist and writer

Lydia Maria Child *(1802–1880)* — American abolitionist and suffragist

Agatha Christie *(1890–1976)* — English writer

Winston Churchill *(1874–1965)* — British statesman and prime minister

Cicero *(106–43 B.C.)* — Roman statesman, orator, and writer

Arthur C. Clarke *(1917–2008)* — English writer

Bill Clinton *(b. 1946)* — 42nd President of the United States

Hillary Clinton *(b. 1947)* — American politician, former U.S. Secretary of State, and former First Lady of the United States

Samuel Taylor Coleridge *(1772–1834)* — English poet, critic, and philosopher

Confucius *(551–479 B.C.)* — Chinese philosopher

Marie Curie *(1867–1934)* — French-Polish physicist and chemist

Dalai Lama (Tenzin Gyatso) *(b. 1935)* — Tibetan monk and religious leader

Paul Davies *(b. 1946)* — British physicist and astrobiologist

Dorothy Day *(1897–1980)* — American journalist and activist

Simone de Beauvoir *(1908–1986)* — French writer, philosopher, and activist

Charles de Gaulle *(1890–1970)* — French general and politician

St. Francis de Sales *(1567–1622)* — French bishop, missionary, and Doctor of the Church

Alexis de Tocqueville *(1805–1859)* — French social philosopher and political theorist

Eugene V. Debs *(1855–1926)* — American union leader and politician

René Descartes *(1596–1650)* — French mathematician and philosopher

John Dewey *(1859–1952)* — American philosopher and educator

Charles Dickens *(1812–1870)* — English writer and social critic

Emily Dickinson *(1830–1886)* — American poet

Benjamin Disraeli *(1804–1881)* — British politician, writer, and prime minister

Fyodor Dostoevsky *(1821–1881)* — Russian novelist

Frederick Douglass *(1818–1895)* — American orator, writer, and activist

W. E. B. Du Bois *(1868–1963)* — American sociologist, educator, and writer

John Foster Dulles *(1888–1959)* — Former U.S. Secretary of State

Alexandre Dumas *(1802–1870)* — French novelist and playwright

Bob Dylan *(b. 1941)* — American singer-songwriter

Freeman Dyson *(b. 1923)* — English-born American theoretical physicist and mathematician

Thomas Edison *(1847–1931)* — American inventor and businessman

Albert Einstein *(1879–1955)* — German-born American physicist

Dwight D. Eisenhower *(1890–1969)* — American general and 34th President of the United States

George Eliot (Mary Ann Evans) *(1819–1880)* — English novelist

T. S. Eliot *(1888–1965)* — American-born English poet, writer, and critic

Ralph Waldo Emerson *(1803–1882)* — American essayist and poet

Epictetus *(c. 55–135 A.D.)* — Greek sage

Euripides *(c. 480–c. 406 B.C.)* — Greek dramatist

Gustave Flaubert *(1821–1880)* — French writer

Malcolm Forbes *(1919–1990)* — American publisher and business leader

Henry Ford *(1863–1947)* — American industrialist and the founder of the Ford Motor Company

E. M. Forster *(1879–1970)* — British writer and critic

Pope Francis *(b. 1936)* — 266th pope of the Catholic Church

Anne Frank *(1929–1945)* — German-born diarist

Benjamin Franklin *(1706–1790)* — American statesman, philosopher, inventor, scientist, and writer

Sigmund Freud *(1856–1939)* — Czech-born Austrian neurologist, known as father of psychoanalysis

Erich Fromm *(1900–1980)* — German-born social psychologist, psychoanalyst, sociologist, and philosopher

Robert Frost *(1874–1963)* — American poet

J. William Fulbright *(1905–1995)* — American politician and statesman

Margaret Fuller *(1810–1850)* — American journalist and critic

R. Buckminster Fuller *(1895–1983)* — American architect, writer, designer, and inventor

John Kenneth Galbraith *(1908–2006)* — American economist

Galileo Galilei *(1564–1642)* — Italian astronomer, physicist, engineer, philosopher, and mathematician

Indira Gandhi *(1917–1984)* — Indian leader and activist

Mahatma Gandhi *(1869–1948)* — Indian nationalist leader and activist

Bill Gates *(b. 1955)* — American business magnate, philanthropist, investor, and inventor

Paul Gauguin *(1848–1903)* — French post-Impressionist artist

A. Bartlett Giamatti *(1938–1989)* — American academic and seventh Commissioner of Major League Baseball

Ruth Bader Ginsburg *(b. 1933)* — American jurist

Nikki Giovanni *(b. 1943)* — American poet and writer, activist, and educator

Malcolm Gladwell *(b. 1963)* — Canadian journalist, writer, and speaker

(Johann Wolfgang von) Goethe *(1749–1832)* — German poet and dramatist

Jane Goodall *(b. 1934)* — British primatologist, ethologist, anthropologist, and activist

Doris Kearns Goodwin *(b. 1943)* — American biographer, historian, and political commentator

Mikhail Gorbachev *(b. 1931)* — Russian politician and social activist

Stephen Jay Gould *(1941–2002)* — American paleontologist, evolutionary biologist, historian of science, and science writer

Maxine Greene *(1917–2014)* — American educational philosopher, writer, teacher, and activist

Germaine Greer *(b. 1939)* — Australian writer and activist

Alexander Hamilton *(1755–1804)* — American statesman

Stephen Hawking *(b. 1942)* — English theoretical physicist, cosmologist, and writer

Nathaniel Hawthorne *(1804–1864)* — American novelist

Georg Hegel *(1770–1831)* — German philosopher

Heraclitus *(c. 535–c. 475 B.C.)* — Greek philosopher

Herodotus *(c. 484–425 B.C.)* — Greek historian

Abraham Joshua Heschel *(1907–1972)* — Polish-born American rabbi and theologian

Hermann Hesse *(1877–1962)* — German-born Swiss poet, novelist, and painter

Thomas Hobbes *(1588–1679)* — English philosopher

Oliver Wendell Holmes, Sr. *(1809–1894)* — American physician, writer, and academic

Horace *(65–8 B.C.)* — Roman poet

David Hume *(1711–1776)* — Scottish philosopher, historian, and economist

John Hume *(b. 1937)* — Irish politician

Zora Neale Hurston *(1891–1960)* — American writer and anthropologist

Aldous Huxley *(1894–1963)* — English writer and philosopher

T. H. Huxley *(1825–1895)* — English biologist

Robert G. Ingersoll *(1833–1899)* — American lawyer, politician, and orator

John Jay *(1745–1829)* — American statesman, diplomat, and jurist

Julian Jaynes *(1920–1987)* — American psychologist and writer

Thomas Jefferson *(1743–1826)* — 3rd President of the United States

Steve Jobs *(1955–2011)* — American entrepreneur, visionary, and inventor

Pope John Paul II *(1920–2005)* — 264th pope of the Catholic Church

Lyndon B. Johnson *(1908–1973)* — 36th President of the United States

Samuel Johnson *(1709–1784)* — English lexicographer, critic, and writer

Ben Jonson *(1572–1637)* — English playwright and poet

Joseph Joubert *(1754–1824)* — French writer and moralist

Carl Jung *(1875–1961)* — Swiss psychologist

Juvenal *(d. 130 A.D.)* — Roman poet

Pauline Kael *(1919–2001)* — American film critic

Franz Kafka *(1883–1924)* — Czech-born German-language novelist

Frida Kahlo *(1907–1954)* — Mexican painter

Daniel Kahneman *(b. 1934)* — Israeli-American psychologist, writer, and academic

Michio Kaku *(b. 1947)* — American futurist, theoretical physicist, and science writer

Immanuel Kant *(1724–1804)* — German philosopher

Helen Keller *(1880–1968)* — American writer, activist, and educator

John F. Kennedy *(1917–1963)* — 35th President of the United States

Nikita Khrushchev *(1894–1971)* — Russian politician

Martin Luther King, Jr. *(1929–1968)* — American clergyman and civil rights leader

Aung San Suu Kyi *(b. 1945)* — Burmese political activist

Diogenes Laërtius *(3rd century B.C.)* — Greek biographer of philosophers

Anne Lamott *(b. 1954)* — American novelist and non-fiction writer

Robert E. Lee *(1807–1870)* — American military officer and general of the Confederate Army during the Civil War

John Lennon *(1940–1980)* — English singer-songwriter

Leonardo da Vinci *(1452–1519)* — Italian painter, sculptor, architect, and engineer

Doris Lessing *(1919–2013)* — English writer

C. S. Lewis *(1898–1963)* — English literary scholar

Abraham Lincoln *(1809–1865)* — 16th President of the United States

John Locke *(1632–1704)* — English philosopher

Audre Lorde *(1934–1992)* — American writer and activist

Martin Luther *(1483–1546)* — German Reformation leader

James Madison *(1751–1836)* — 4th President of the United States

Malcolm X *(1925–1965)* — American religious leader and activist

Nelson Mandela *(1918–2013)* — South African political leader, activist, humanitarian, philanthropist, and lawyer

Karl Marx *(1818–1883)* — German political philosopher and socialist

Mary McCarthy *(1912–1989)* — American writer, critic, and activist

Paul McCartney *(b. 1942)* — English singer-songwriter and composer

David McCullough *(b. 1933)* — American writer, historian, narrator, and lecturer

Margaret Mead *(1901–1978)* — American cultural anthropologist and writer

Mencius *(c. 372–289 B.C.)* — Chinese philosopher

Angela Merkel *(b. 1954)* — German politician

Thomas Merton *(1915–1968)* — American religious writer

Michelangelo (Michelangelo di Lodovico Buonarroti Simoni)
   (1475–1564) — Italian sculptor, painter, architect, poet, and engineer

John Stuart Mill *(1806–1873)* — English philosopher and economist

Arthur Miller *(1915–2005)* — American playwright and essayist

Henry Miller *(1891–1980)* — American writer

Montaigne (Michel de Montaigne) *(1533–1592)* — French essayist

Maria Montessori *(1870–1952)* — Italian physician and educator

Toni Morrison *(b. 1931)* — American novelist, editor, and professor

Elon Musk *(b. 1971)* — South African–born business magnate, engineer,
   inventor, and investor

Pablo Neruda *(1904–1973)* — Chilean poet, diplomat, and politician

Sir Isaac Newton *(1643–1727)* — English physicist and mathematician

Reinhold Niebuhr *(1892–1971)* — American theologian, political
   commentator, and academic

Friedrich Nietzsche *(1844–1900)* — German philosopher

Anaïs Nin *(1903–1977)* — French-born American writer

Henri Nouwen *(1932–1996)* — Dutch religious writer and theologian

Flannery O'Connor *(1925–1964)* — American writer

Georgia O'Keeffe *(1887–1986)* — American painter

Joyce Carol Oates *(b. 1938)* — American writer

Barack Obama *(b. 1961)* — 44th President of the United States

Ovid *(b. 43 B.C.)* — Roman poet

Camille Paglia *(b. 1947)* — American writer, academic, and social critic

Thomas Paine *(1737–1809)* — English-born American politician, philosopher,
   and writer

Blaise Pascal *(1623–1662)* — French mathematician, philosopher, and scientist

Octavio Paz *(1914–1998)* — Mexican poet and essayist

Pericles *(495–429 B.C.)* — Greek statesman, orator, and general

Pablo Picasso *(1881–1973)* — Spanish-born artist, sculptor, poet, and
   playwright

Steven Pinker *(b. 1954)* — Canadian-born American cognitive scientist, psychologist, linguist, professor, and writer

Plato *(c. 428–c. 348 B.C.)* — Greek philosopher and writer

Plutarch *(c. 46–c. 122 A.D.)* — Greek philosopher and writer

Alexander Pope *(1688–1744)* — English poet

Marcel Proust *(1871–1922)* — French novelist, essayist, and critic

Ayn Rand *(1905–1982)* — Russian-born American writer

Rembrandt (van Rijn) *(1606–1669)* — Dutch painter and etcher

Rainer Maria Rilke *(1875–1926)* — Bohemian-Austrian poet and novelist

Auguste Rodin *(1840–1917)* — French sculptor

Eleanor Roosevelt *(1884–1962)* — American humanitarian, political activist, and longest-serving First Lady of the United States

Franklin D. Roosevelt *(1882–1945)* — 32nd President of the United States and the only president elected four times

Theodore Roosevelt *(1858–1919)* — 26th President of the United States

Edward Rothstein *(b. 1952)* — American music critic and composer

Jean-Jacques Rousseau *(1712–1778)* — Swiss-born French philosopher, writer, and composer

Salman Rushdie *(b. 1947)* — Indian-British writer

Bertrand Russell *(1872–1970)* — British philosopher and mathematician

Oliver Sacks *(1933–2015)* — British-born neurologist, naturalist, and writer

Carl Sagan *(1934–1996)* — American astronomer, cosmologist, astrophysicist, astrobiologist, and writer

George Sand *(1804–1876)* — French writer

George Santayana *(1863–1952)* — American philosopher and poet

Jean-Paul Sartre *(1905–1980)* — French philosopher, writer, and activist

Charles M. Schulz *(1922–2000)* — American cartoonist

Albert Schweitzer *(1875–1965)* — German-French theologian, philosopher, missionary, and physician

Seneca *(c. 4 B.C.–65 A.D.)* — Roman philosopher, statesman, and dramatist

William Shakespeare *(1564–1616)* — English poet, playwright, and actor

George Bernard Shaw *(1856–1950)* — Irish-born British writer

Socrates *(470–399 B.C.)* — Greek philosopher

Aleksandr Solzhenitsyn *(1918–2008)* — Russian novelist, historian, and political activist

Sonia Sotomayor *(b. 1954)* — American jurist

Thomas Sowell *(b. 1930)* — American economist, political philosopher, and writer

Herbert Spencer *(1820–1903)* — English philosopher and sociologist

Benedict de Spinoza *(1632–1677)* — Dutch philosopher

Elizabeth Cady Stanton *(1815–1902)* — American social activist, abolitionist, and pioneer of the U.S. women's rights movement

Gertrude Stein *(1874–1946)* — American writer and literary innovator

John Steinbeck *(1902–1968)* — American novelist

Gloria Steinem *(b. 1934)* — American writer, journalist, and political and social activist

Robert Louis Stevenson *(1850–1894)* — Scottish novelist, poet, and essayist

Igor Stravinsky *(1882–1971)* — Russian-born composer, pianist, and conductor

Jonathan Swift *(1667–1745)* — Anglo-Irish political satirist, writer, and cleric

Terence Tao *(b. 1975)* — Australian-born Chinese-American mathematician

Mother Teresa *(1910–1997)* — Albanian-born Roman Catholic nun and missionary

William Makepeace Thackeray *(1811–1863)* — English novelist, poet, and satirist

William Thomson, Lord Kelvin *(1824–1907)* — English physicist and mathematician

Henry David Thoreau *(1817–1862)* — American philosopher, writer, and naturalist

Leo Tolstoy *(1828–1910)* — Russian novelist and philosopher

Harry S. Truman *(1884–1972)* — 33rd President of the United States

Barbara Tuchman *(1912–1989)* — American writer and historian

Desmond Tutu *(b. 1931)* — South African social rights activist and retired Anglican bishop

Mark Twain *(1835–1910)* — American writer and humorist

Neil deGrasse Tyson *(b. 1958)* — American astrophysicist, cosmologist, and science writer

Lao Tzu *(c. 604–531 B.C.)* — Chinese philosopher and poet

John Updike *(1932–2009)* — American writer and critic

Voltaire *(1694–1778)* — French philosopher and writer

Otto von Bismarck *(1815–1898)* — Prussian statesman

Friedrich August von Hayek *(1899–1992)* — Austro-Hungarian-born economist and philosopher

Alice Walker *(b. 1944)* — American novelist, poet, and activist

Earl Warren *(1891–1974)* — American jurist, politician, and Chief Justice of the Supreme Court

Booker T. Washington *(1856–1915)* — American educator, writer, activist, and most prominent African-American leader of his time

George Washington *(1732–1799)* — 1st President of the United States

Simone Weil *(1909–1943)* — French philosopher, mystic, and activist

Ai Weiwei *(b. 1957)* — Chinese artist and activist

H. G. Wells *(1866–1946)* — English writer

Cornel West *(b. 1953)* — American philosopher, professor, writer, and activist

Edith Wharton *(1862–1937)* — American novelist

Alfred North Whitehead *(1861–1947)* — English mathematician and philosopher

Walt Whitman *(1819–1892)* — American poet

Elie Wiesel *(b. 1928)* — Romanian-born American writer, professor, political activist, and humanitarian

Oscar Wilde *(1854–1900)* — Irish writer

Woodrow Wilson *(1856–1924)* — 28th President of the United States

Ludwig Wittgenstein *(1889–1951)* — Austrian-British philosopher and academic

Mary Wollstonecraft *(1757–1797)* — English writer, philosopher, and activist

Virginia Woolf *(1882–1941)* — English writer

William Wordsworth *(1770–1850)* — English poet

Frank Lloyd Wright *(1867–1959)* — American architect, interior designer, writer, and educator

William Butler Yeats *(1865–1939)* — Irish poet